Gifted for Good

Gifted for Good

Every Woman's Guide to Her Spiritual Gifts

Kathryn Deering

SERVANT PUBLICATIONS
ANN ARBOR, MICHIGAN

Vine Books is an imprint of Servant Publications especially designed to serve evangelical Christians.

Names and other details of the personal stories in this book may have been changed to protect privacy where necessary. Stories employing actual names and details have been used with explicit written permission.

Published by Servant Publications
P.O. Box 8617
Ann Arbor, Michigan 48107

Cover design: Paul Higdon

00 01 02 03 10 9 8 7 6 5 4 3 2 1

Printed in the United States of America
ISBN 1-56955-089-1

Library of Congress Cataloging-in-Publication Data

Deering, Kathryn, 1949-
Gifted for good : every woman's guide to her spiritual gifts / Kathryn Deering.
p. cm.
Includes bibliographical references.
ISBN 1-56955-089-1 (alk. paper)
1. Christian women—Religious life. 2. Gifts, Spiritual. I. Title.
BV4527.D44 2000
234'.13'082—dc21 00-020906

Dear Cookie
May God's love always guide you in the discovery and use of the gifts He has granted you.

Love,
Juliette

Lovingly dedicated to the four Deerings
who are God's special gifts to me:
Liz, Jim, Laura, and Christy.
I'm so glad to be your mom!

Contents

Acknowledgments

Special thanks to the many women whose names appear in this book. You are godly women.

Extra credit to:

- Priscilla Dunning for her expertise and synergistic zeal.
- Bert Ghezzi and Gwen Ellis for giving the green light to this project, and Heidi Hess Saxton for carrying it to completion.
- Miriam Seaver for her editorial eye and for using her gift of teaching to field-test the gift definitions.
- The members of Miriam's Bible study, Cindy, Amy, Christi, and Rita, for their helpful feedback.
- Mark Vanderput for his theological help and for being such a fine pastor—and for planting the seed of this idea in the first place.
- My extraordinary husband, Mike, whose gifts and talents make him far more than "just a husband."

Part I:

You Were Meant for Significance

As a Christian woman, you know you are supposed to be a possessor of something called "abundant life." Yet many of us, assured for many years that we are heaven-bound, sigh, "Is that all there is?"

Abundant life is not the same as material wealth, regardless of what advertising would have us believe. Abundant life involves being truly fulfilled by finding God's will for our lives and doing what we were born to do.

Are you doing what you were born to do? Do you like what you're doing? Have you found your special niche in the body of Christ? Do you think your life has borne fruit in the lives of others? Discovering your spiritual gifts and using them are integral elements in finding the joy of abundant life.

Spiritual gifts help you define your identity. You are not "just a housewife," or "a student," or even "the first female president of XYZ, Inc." You are a daughter of the King of heaven, born into an inheritance that includes, here and now—before heaven—the grace to live a new life. Part of your new life in Christ is expressed through your spiritual gifts, which I like to call "re-birthday presents."

Your spiritual gifts weren't presented to you wrapped in pretty paper, although figuratively speaking they may be under wraps even to this day. Just as you need physical fingers with which to open the paper wrappings of birthday presents, you need the "fingers" of God's Holy Spirit, who has been given to each of us as believers, to unwrap your spiritual birthday presents. This book can help you to see God's Spirit at work in you.

God's gifts to humankind have not been labelled "For Men Only" or "For Women Only" any more than they've been reserved for certain age groups or people with specific education levels. However, I have observed that we women often discover and use our spiritual gifts in distinctly feminine ways.

For example, women are more likely than men to talk and read about personal issues. We like to learn about our relationships and how experiences affect them. We want to understand ourselves better. We tend to observe how people "tick." Learning about our own highly personal spiritual gifts is part of learning more about ourselves and how we can relate best to the people around us.

We women thrive when encouragement and reassurance are served up with a garnish of specific details. If I ask my husband, "How do I look in this dress?" I want more than his "Fine." I want *particulars:* Does he like the color, style, length? Does it make me look fatter or thinner? Younger, maybe?

I want the same kind of human touch when I learn about spiritual gifts. Not too much analysis, too many graphs, or too much theologizing, please; I prefer to hear about real-people details. This isn't just a personal quirk; research results consistently show that, as a group, women pay greater attention to such details than men do. We are encouraged and instructed by them. I wrote this book with this observation in mind.

Even if "finding your niche" sounds inviting, you may feel concerned about time. How are you going to pause your life long enough to find that niche? Maybe you feel you're already up to capacity. Sure, the local grocery store is open twenty-four hours to serve you, but somehow that hasn't improved the quality of your life. You're managing to look after things from day to day, but not exactly shopping around for more to do. Do you dare read the rest of this book?

Yes! If you want a new way to streamline your busy life, read on. As you develop your spiritual gifts, your energy can become better focused and your satisfaction can increase. Abundant life does not mean a too-busy life.

Up to Our Hips in Books

In the past three decades, so many books (and pamphlets and magazine articles) have been published on the subject of spiritual gifts that it is probably humanly impossible to obtain all of them. Besides printed matter, Christians have been provided with numerous conferences and classes in their churches, small groups, and seminaries.

Why add another book to the pile? Why did I bother to write this book?

For you. For the woman who, like myself, can't exactly see herself in the example of the fellow profiled in her church spiritual-gifts seminar. You know, the gifted guy (pastor, often) who has conducted a phenomenally successful evangelistic crusade, complete with documented healings. Even if you have similar gifts of healing and evangelism, there's no way *you* can hit the sawdust trail. The dog just had puppies, and the minivan is in the shop....

Or you hear about the successful Christian businessman who has decided to give so much of his money away that some people say he's generous to a fault. He has the "gift of giving," others say. It makes you wonder if little ol' you could ever possibly have the same gift, clutching your cents-off coupons at the grocery store on Tuesday morning after you've worked the night shift at the hospital.

Although bazillions of books have been written for and about women (especially since the 1970s), very little on *this* subject has been directed specifically to us as women. Most of the information about spiritual gifts, logically enough, has been presented by men (often pastors) with the whole body of Christ in mind. It's good stuff, by and large. I'll be referring to lots of it throughout this book.

Less press. I'm not blaming men for somehow letting us down. I've taken this women-only approach because it's a simple fact of church history that women haven't gotten as much press. Think about the women described in the New Testament, none of whom wrote a word of it. They are mostly *receiving* miracles, not administering them. Or they are behind the scenes, serving (think of Martha, Peter's mother-in-law, or Dorcas), and you need to read between the lines to see their gifts.

Christian women have not been somehow less gifted than the men—they just haven't been the ones holding the pen as often. That can put us at a subtle disadvantage as we search out our particular niches in the body of Christ. I don't want to waste time being irritated about it; I do want to do my bit to remedy that disadvantage in a practical, "For Women Only," way.

Just think of this book as sort of a coach, or a collection of coaches. We all need coaches to help us run the race of our new life in Christ. In past generations, women more often lived in cohesive, extended family situations. The presence of older female relatives lent itself to natural coaching or mentoring. Without any of today's elaborate tests or gift surveys, many a Christian woman could discover and use her gifts because Mother or Grandmother or Aunt Agnes encouraged her. Think of this book as your Aunt Agnes.

I will give you an overview and some background on the subject of spiritual gifts in the first few chapters, but my goal in this book is to bring to life—for you as a woman—the gifts of the Holy Spirit. In these pages you will meet real-life women from all walks of life. You will see how they discovered their gifts and how they use them. You will be surprised to see the wide variety represented in these pages. I know it will expand your horizons; it has mine.

No Woman Is an Island

To help me collect enough true stories and to give me a hearty leg up on the whole topic of women and spiritual gifts, I enlisted the assistance of Priscilla Dunning, who has been teaching and mentoring women on the subject for twenty years. In our own gifts and personalities, we are quite different. It has been a delightful arrangement because we so perfectly illustrate the principle of complementarity as it operates in the body of Christ. The gifts and personality traits I have lacked, Priss has had, and vice versa.

We aren't opposites in everything, however. One thing we have in common is a desire to see all Christian women walking in their full inheritance from God. Over the years, we have wished for a practical, "how-to" resource for our own sakes and for the sake of the women we serve, a resource that would address the subject of spiritual giftedness through a distinctly feminine looking glass. Other women in women's ministries have expressed the same need.

So here is that resource. It's an overview of the spiritual gifts described in the New Testament, liberally illustrated with real-life examples of *women* in action. If your life circumstances have kept you so swamped that you didn't have time for that spiritual-gifts seminar anyway, maybe this book will be just right for you.

One

Eureka!

You might do the usual things: finish school, get married, have a couple of children. Things may go along smoothly or they may blow up in your face. For Myra Ricksaller, they blew up.

First, her husband abandoned her. In her small midwestern town in the early 1960s, she didn't even know of one other woman in her predicament. She had two girls to support, no job, and no particular job skills. Anyway, there weren't that many paying jobs in her farming community.

Both of her parents had died, and her brother and sister, although their families lived nearby, had always maintained a "you live your life and I'll live mine" approach to family relationships. Myra was on her own.

As she regained her footing after the initial shock, she talked with her daughters, Judy, then ten, and Nancy, eight. "We're in this together, girls. I'm going to need you to pitch in all you can."

The first year was the worst. Myra had to apply for public assistance, which was demeaning to her. She struggled to get through each day, becoming steadily more and more depressed. Her husband seemed to have vanished without a trace.

That summer, her daughters were invited to a vacation Bible school at the only church in town, a Methodist church. Although Myra had never attended church much, she figured it might brighten their summer, so she let them go. Parents were invited to a closing program of music and skits.

Judy and Nancy greeted their mom eagerly, pressing up against her. "Come way up front, please, Mom. We want you to see us!"

The last skit was a dialogue between a Christian and a searcher. Judy was playing the part of the searcher. Somehow, watching her own daughter ask hard questions about God brought it all into focus for Myra. By the end of the skit, she had decided to become a Christian.

Her decision had a dramatic effect on her sense of helplessness. Myra's sense of worth and hope increased almost daily. Church members reached out to her and to the girls. One of them was a retired school administrator, and he encouraged Myra to go back to school. "Think about it and pray," he said, "God will help you find just the right training and job."

The cosmetology school in the next county was not the greatest, but they did have a deferred tuition program; you could take enough classes to learn the rudiments and then start to work off your debt in their storefront shop. Myra realized she always had liked fixing people's hair. She decided to commute to school while there was still life left in the old car.

After passing the licensing exam, and with the help of one of her church friends who co-signed a loan with her, she opened Myra's Beauty Shoppe in the walk-out basement of her home. Life was looking up.

Several years later, when the girls were finishing high school, Myra saw a TV exposé about the women's prison in a city thirty miles away. The prison drew its inmates from the entire state, and conditions were not good. Myra saw women being separated from their toddlers and infants. In the overcrowded cells, a wild-looking woman who had murdered her boyfriend's child was bunked with five others who had committed lesser offenses. All of them endured dim lighting, primitive toilets, and group showers that looked to Myra more like gas chambers in Nazi concentration camps.

Something inside her cried out, "I was in prison and you visited me!" She trembled at the idea that God might be calling her to go to these women, but by now she had had enough experience at hearing his still, small voice to realize that this might indeed be a specific call from him.

She talked with her girls. "You can't just *go* to the prison, Mom!" Judy remonstrated. "I think you have to be somebody with a relative there, or a minister maybe."

"Yes, probably you're right." She didn't know who to ask anyway.

A few months later, there was another TV report on the prison. This time there had been a food fight in the dining hall, and it had turned ugly. Myra thought her heart would jump through her throat.

She began to pray in earnest, "Lord, show me if this is you. Please, if it is you, show me what to do. Before, I didn't even know there was a women's prison so close, but now I just want to reach out to them somehow...."

That week, Myra awoke one morning with a germ of an idea. "I'll volunteer my services as a hairdresser!" she thought excitedly. "Maybe they already have somebody to do it, but maybe they don't."

It wasn't long before her Monday prison visit became the highlight of Myra's week. She gave "easy-care" haircuts, shampoos, and most of all, much-needed attention. Under her gentle hands, women opened up.

She heard some hair-raising stories! More often they were heartbreaking ones. The wardens let her help the women in other ways, simple but so important. She phoned relatives, "Please come visit ____. She's lonely." She arranged for birthday and Christmas gifts to be purchased and delivered to inmates' children.

Back home, her Tuesday through Saturday clients heard about Myra's adventures. Because of Myra's love and enthusiasm, they could feel a sympathetic bond with the women in prison. They dropped spare change into the can Myra kept on the counter for donations to cover her prison supplies. Some of them, who were Myra's friends from church, started pitching in on some of the outside efforts, especially at Christmastime.

Now almost seventy, Myra has retired from her home business. She devotes most of her time to her prison work. So often, she says, "Hardened hearts are softened by my simple kindness. It's a taste of God's mercy, I guess. These ladies know they haven't earned such kindness. Then when other Christian prison volunteers come into the facility with their gifts for Bible teaching, a lot of those softer hearts are ready to come to Jesus. I guess I'm just the soil waterer who gets the soil ready for the good seed. But even if none of them had ever become Christians, I would have done the same thing."

In prison, of all places, Myra found her purpose in life. She is a happy woman. She discovered the Lord of her life *and* the

* See the appendix for detailed gift definitions.

perfect "fit" for her spiritual gifts of mercy and helps.* Other Christians came alongside her, exercising their gifts of teaching and evangelism (VBS staff and other prison volunteers), wisdom and shepherding/ pastoring (the retired school administrator), giving (her clients), and many more.

I Have Found It!

Not all of us will feel directly guided as Myra did. But we too can have "eureka!" experiences—if we prayerfully seek God's will for our lives.

Eureka is Greek for "I have found [it]!" It's an exclamation of triumph, associated with Archimedes, who purportedly said it when he discovered how to ascertain the purity of gold. Both by traditional association and by simple meaning, the word has special significance for us as we seek to find the purest possible expression of our spiritual gifts.

Leslie Flynn calls this the "'delight' criterion." He considers it to be equivalent to the "peace" criterion for which we look when we are seeking God's will.[1] In spiritual and personal terms, eureka delight means, "This, really, is what I would rather do for God than anything else in the world."[2] The overflow of delight gives us energy. It is contagious, often helping us to lead others into the discovery of similar gifts.

No longer do we feel like square pegs in round holes. Finally, it all makes sense. Our life experiences, both good and bad, and our spiritual gifts, which may have seemed inadequate, fit together.

How do we each arrive at a personal "eureka moment"?

The discovery process follows this pattern: (1) Experiment,

(2) Evaluate, (3) Expect confirmation.[3] A fourth "E" would be—you guessed it—"Eureka!"

Experiment. Experimenting with various roles is a lot like trying on shoes or clothes. Try them on until you find some that fit and coordinate with your other characteristics.

Most of us do this automatically. We gravitate toward the roles about which we feel the most positive. I might discover that I'm not much good at, say, organizing a series of church dinners, but that I really don't mind throwing a spontaneous barbecue for the adult choir. In terms of spiritual gifts, I might begin to conclude that I don't have the gifts of administration, leadership, or service, but that I really do have a gift of hospitality.

Be somewhat adventuresome, but be practical too. What works? Are you lousy at teaching children? Try teaching a women's Bible study. Not so good at that, either? Maybe hospitality is a stronger gift than teaching for you. See if another woman would like to lead it while you host it. Or perhaps your teaching gift is not meant for the classroom. Yours could be a behind-the-scenes gift best suited for writing scripts for a radio teaching ministry.

Perhaps family responsibilities currently prevent you from doing much of any "church work," but you find yourself drawn to pray for others when you are up in the middle of the night with an invalid or your baby. Try intercession on for size. Learn more about how you can best do it.

Evaluate. Fifteen-year-old Lori was asked to teach crafts at her church's day camp. She had always liked handicrafts. An elderly family friend was teaching her the art of tatting. Lori had often contributed salable items to the annual missions fund-raising bazaar and had always helped her mom decorate the social hall for the annual church father-son banquet. She could easily identify her creativity and artistic talent. But what spiritual gifts could be hiding in Lori? What other patterns could she see?

How about teaching? (*Lori, do you like to explain the crafts as clearly as possible? Do you sometimes find yourself building little spiritual lessons into the crafts projects?*) Exhortation or shepherding? (*Lori, do you like to identify and bring out the best in each child? Do you feel protective of them?*) Leadership? (*Lori, do kids like to follow you? Does it feel natural to take charge if nobody else does?*)

Or—most likely of all—is it a nice Lori-blend? Lori could be gifted with all of the above, including a dash of hospitality, a pinch of helps, and a garnish of intercession that enables Lori to pray for the projects and people. As she grows up, she may discover other gifts that aren't obvious yet, because Lori has not had enough years to experiment widely.

Sometimes evaluation can be a bit confusing. Cindy, a woman in my church, knew that she felt uncomfortable showing hospitality, yet she always seemed to end up volunteering to do just that. One day she figured out that her strong gift of helps motivated her to volunteer for lots of duties, many of which included hospitality. Now she can give herself credit for being a marvelous helper in spite of her little dip in the hospitality department.

Think about your church-related activities. Think about what you do on weekends. How about at work? List half a dozen instances where you found satisfaction and fulfillment in an activity. Ask someone you know to help you see a pattern in your list.

You might find that most of what you are doing is *not* satisfying or fulfilling in any way. What then? Whenever you are evaluating yourself, remember: "You are not the wrong person. You are the right person, but may be in the wrong position."[4] Even a negative evaluation has much value. It will help steer you in the right direction and enhance the delight of your "eureka moment" when it comes.

Expect confirmation. If Lori begins to wonder if she has any of the spiritual gifts listed above, she can be on the lookout for informal confirmation. Parents may say, "Lori, thank you! Your craft project helped Susie comprehend the Sunday-school lesson as never before!" or, "Lori, the kids follow you as if you're the Pied Piper! How do you do it?" Or, simply, "Lori, you look so happy when you're doing that."

Lori's best confirmations may come from others who possess similar gifts. One of the signs of a gift in our lives is that the longer we live the more we will recognize the same gift in other Christians. We will be excited about that gift and we will want to see it used widely. Prophets will want to encourage other prophets, and so on for all the gifts.

Many of us will find that we have already discovered our spiritual gifts through our working relationships with others, without ever bothering to apply gift names or categories to what we do. We are successfully and happily serving. Our personal "eureka" may be the confirmation that our hidden role has a name, that what we are doing has particular value in the sight of God.

Take initiative. Don't just wait for discovery to happen—put yourself in the pathway of discovery. Take a few risks in your experimentation. Don't be like that servant who kept his funds buried because he didn't want to take the risk (see Mt 25:14-30). Whatever works, do more of it.

Ask God to guide your prayers about gifts. Paul urged the Corinthians to pray for gifts (see 1 Cor 14:13). If you have the gift of tongues, pray for the gift of interpretation. If you have the gift of leadership, pray (oh, please!) for the gift of wisdom to go with it.

Explore new ideas. Read more about spiritual gifts. Take advantage of less-threatening settings such as comfortable small groups or anonymous large conferences. Listen to others who are good at something you would like to do.

Impatient with your discovery progress? Let your impatience motivate you to more prayer. Let God lead you to another step.

What About Gift Tests?

Most of us are aware of one or more written tests that have been devised to help Christians discover their spiritual gifts. Why not start with one of those?

Well, for one reason, because we can only answer a gift test well if we've already been doing some experimenting, with feedback from others. Fellow Christians are our mirrors. We can only know ourselves to the degree that others have accurately reflected us back; tests and questionnaires help us make sense of that feedback. Discovery of our giftedness is more hindsight than foresight.

If you're a brand-new Christian, it makes even more sense to postpone a gift test until later. You need to have been an active participant in a local church to have a basis for answering the questions on a spiritual gifts questionnaire.

Testing for spiritual gifts is not a science. No spiritual-gifts test is perfect, and no such test will convey God's final word to you. Spiritual-gifts tests are designed only to help you detect the observable patterns in your life.

The Resources section in the back of this book can direct you to several types of tests. One of the best-known tests for spiritual gifts was modified by C. Peter Wagner from an earlier test known as the Houts test.[5] The Wagner-Modified Houts Questionnaire contains 125 questions which can help Christians get a handle on their spiritual gifts.[6]

Many gifts tests have been modified from the Houts test to fit with various denominational specifications. Others have been devised from scratch. Some teachers have posted their efforts on the Internet.

As noted earlier, spiritual gifts teachers have assembled gift lists that vary. For instance, instead of the list I am using, some resources refer to "motivational gifts."[7] The resources section of this book includes more than one approach.

Perhaps you can start with the Spiritual Gifts Survey for Women in the appendix. Do take some sort of spiritual gifts test as a part of your evaluation process.

For Further Discussion

Additional information can help you better apply your spiritual gifts in a way that suits both your personality and sense of calling. Discovering your spiritual gifts helps you know *what* you should do. Finding out, for instance, about your personality and working style helps you know *how* you can best do it. Considering your "passion"[8] (other words for which might be *burden, dream, vision,* or *call)* guides you to *where* you can serve most happily.

To discover more about how you tick and to provide yourself with a springboard for further discovery, take an interest/preference survey or a personality profile.[9] See if you can better figure out why you're restless in your current job. Do the requirements of the job match your personal qualities? Evaluate your working style. Are you an organizer, or do you need others to organize your workload for you? How do you arrive at decisions? How much do you need other people? Are you an introvert or an extrovert or both? Let test results give you some new vocabulary with which to describe yourself. (Be discerning. Sometimes these tools are used in schools or in the secular workplace but are based on non-Christian religions, including the "religion" of corporate success.)

Glean new insights from teachings about birth order from experts such as Kevin Leman.[10] You may discover that what you had considered a gift of leadership is less spiritual gift and more bossy big sister!

Ask yourself, "What really excites me?" It could be anything: I would like to help prepare couples for marriage ... lead a weekly worship service in a nursing home ... be a researcher for a Bible translator ... explain the gospel to young Asian students at my local university ... picket at an abortion clinic ... teach ten-year-olds how to make homemade pretzels....

A Few Words of Caution

It might go without saying, but don't expect to find out about your spiritual gifts from a personality test. Conversely, don't try to find out about your personality from a spiritual-gifts test. At the same time, don't assume any test is the final word on your gifts or personality. It's a process of ongoing discovery.

Do be involved with other people, but don't try to copy anyone. You are unique.

Don't let busyness sabotage your efforts. For both introverts (who need plenty of quiet) and extroverts (who thrive on stimulation, but may use activity to anesthetize a feeling of unfulfillment), being too busy prevents self-evaluation.

Don't be discouraged if you find it difficult to understand a test. Your ability to fill out a questionnaire depends on your vocabulary skills, your past experiences (remember it's mostly hindsight), and your level of self-confidence. Perhaps a friend can help you.

Don't let yourself feel inferior if your scores seem low. Your higher scores are meaningful only in relation to your own lower scores—*not* in relation to anybody else's scores. Extravagant Elsie may have given herself three "fifteens" just because she does everything with a flourish. Timid Trish's highest score of "nine" may represent an extraordinary degree of gifting.

Don't despair if your gift mix just does not equip you to do something you really would like to do. You can use the gifts you have to "underwrite" someone else who has the gifts you lack. Remember how Myra's gifts of mercy and helps worked together with others' gifts.

Don't forget to pray. Ask God to help you not only to discover your personal blend of gifts, but to guide you in using them.

After the Dust Has Settled

C. Peter Wagner believes that the ability to discover our spiritual gifts is a function of our emotional maturity.[11] For some, emotional maturity is slowed by difficult life circumstances, and many of us will need help to achieve it. As we grow in other ways, we can be discovering our spiritual gifts too.

Although we can often identify and encourage patterns of giftedness in our children, most Christians will not become very sure of their gifts until they are in their early twenties. Emotional maturity needs to be factored in, plus an accumulation of experience over time.

We change as we mature. Take a spiritual-gifts test again after five or ten years to get an even clearer picture of your strengths. Bear in mind that different gifts will come into prominence at different seasons of your life. More "eurekas" may be in store for you!

In actual fact, the dust never settles! The joy of discovery never stops in our intriguing new life with God.

Two

Gifts Don't Come in Boxes

My collaborator, Priscilla Dunning, chose *Gifts Don't Come in Boxes* as the title for her master's thesis, reusing it as a title for her subsequent presentations at retreats and women's conferences. The words capture a very important concept. While we can call spiritual gifts by specific names and discuss their characteristics in some detail, we just can't force them into tidy pigeonholes and seal them up.

Not that Christians don't try. But we can't even agree on how many "real" spiritual gifts there are. Some insist there are seven,[1] some no more than nine.[2] Many expand the list to twenty-three[3] or twenty-seven.[4] Others stick with nineteen[5] or twenty.[6] All for good reasons.

I'm with Corrie ten Boom, who said, "The Lord did not in any way give His gifts as a means to quarrel about, but He gave His gifts that we should enjoy them."[7] I suspect that just as every plant or body part was not named in the Bible, neither should we assume that every gift has been named there. Why would an infinitely creative God, he who blends the colors of the sunsets, limit us to a handful of sternly delineated gifts?

Unwrapping the Gifts

We can find three lists of spiritual gifts in the Bible (see Rom 12:6-8; 1 Cor 12:28; Eph 4:11), with scattered additional references to them throughout the four Gospels, Acts, 1 Peter, Hebrews, and Paul's epistles. The lists overlap to some extent, but no two match each other gift-for-gift.

Nowhere in the New Testament is there a systematic listing of all the spiritual gifts. We might have found a certain satisfaction in having one authoritative listing of every single spiritual gift, but we just don't have one. This fact alone may be reason enough to conclude that the scriptural gifts are merely a representative sampling of the possible gifts, that the Holy Spirit bestows such a wide variety of blendings and degrees of giftedness that no list could cover them all.

Spiritual gifts operate by spiritual means. They are relatively fluid by definition. "The wind [Spirit] blows where it wills, and you hear the sound of it, but you do not know whence it comes or whither it goes; so it is with every one who is born of the Spirit" (Jn 3:8, RSV). "The letter kills, but the Spirit gives life" (2 Cor 3:6b).

We do need to settle on some serviceable framework in order to discuss spiritual gifts. But we can lapse into legalistic thinking if we become too strict in defining the limits of each gift. One Spirit controls and unifies the whole, but no one human system can codify it. If you are moving with the wind of the Holy Spirit, there is *always* something new and exciting around the next corner!

The Gift Shop

To make the reach of this book as broad as possible, I have relied upon one of the most expanded gift lists, the one that C. Peter Wagner and others have made so widely known since 1979. Wagner, in his classic book, *Your Spiritual Gifts Can Help Your Church Grow,* lists twenty-seven gifts that he feels are explicitly mentioned in the New Testament.[8] They are as follows:

1. Administration
2. Apostle
3. Celibacy
4. Deliverance
5. Discernment of Spirits
6. Evangelism
7. Exhortation
8. Faith
9. Giving
10. Healing
11. Helps
12. Hospitality
13. Intercession
14. Interpretation of Tongues
15. Knowledge
16. Leadership
17. Martyr
18. Mercy
19. Miracles
20. Missionary
21. Shepherd/Pastor
22. Prophecy
23. Service
24. Teaching
25. Tongues
26. Voluntary Poverty
27. Wisdom

I have found the most potential for cooperation with the "wind of the Spirit" by employing this longer list of twenty-seven gifts because it allows for more gift-combination possibilities. A fuller appreciation for the open-endedness of God's creativity can begin with a wider springboard of gifts.

Turn to the appendix for a valuable, concise description of each of these twenty-seven gifts. You may wish to bookmark that section for easy reference throughout the rest of your reading. These particular gift definitions have been written specifically for women by Priscilla Dunning.

Many authors take the gifts mentioned in Scripture and group them in various categories for the sake of easier comprehension.[9] I will not be using any such categorizations overtly, although they often underlie my instinctive grasp of this material. I don't want us to become so focused on compartmentalizing the spiritual gifts that we keep certain gifts at arm's length from each other.

Gifts such as service or helps seem to be more a part of someone's personality than, say, miracles or healing (often called "sign gifts"), which require specific empowering of the Holy Spirit each time the gift is used. However, if we are concentrating too hard on which gifts are "service" gifts and which are "sign" gifts, we might miss the fact that *possessors of sign gifts always have other gifts.* We can't isolate them from each other.

Grace abounding. If you have a spiritual gift, it will be demonstrated in your daily, ordinary service to the people around you. As you are washing a sinkful of dishes someday, you might feel, as my friend Grace Bailey once did, that God wants you drop everything to hop in the car and drive downtown, where you will feel you should pick up a distressed stranger at a bus stop. You might, like Grace, take her to the hospital to see her young son, keep in touch with her afterward, and discover that she lives right across from your church. You might invite her to visit your church, where you will lead her to faith in Jesus as Savior. You might even see the evangelistic miracle multiply many-fold, as Grace did: The woman's older son, who happened to be a gang leader, also became a Christian because of his mother's new faith. He brought his whole gang to church, and they all became fervent believers. They invited their friends too. The church was soon full of new Christians—the woman's entire family plus all those teens—all because of Grace's sensitivity to God's quiet nudge as she was serving her family at the kitchen sink!

Natural and Supernatural

God knows what he's doing when he mixes and blends our spiritual gifts and when he combines our gift mix with our natural personalities and circumstances. Throughout Scripture we see the blends of various spiritual gifts and the God-ordained events of the natural world. Paul is shipwrecked on the stormy beach of Malta (natural event—see Acts 28). A blazing fire of sticks is lit to warm and dry the survivors (also natural). A viper, flushed out of the brushwood Paul was adding to the fire, attaches itself to his hand (entirely natural—and deadly). Paul suffers no ill effects (supernatural miracle) and goes on to work miracles of healing for the amazed islanders. The Holy Spirit is directing every detail.

As we are identifying our own gifts, most of us will focus more intently on them one at a time, as if they were in boxes. Just try to remember to appreciate the bigger picture; your gifts just won't stay in those boxes!

Some of these gifts make some people a little nervous. Your reaction to each gift will be conditioned by your denominational affiliation and past experiences. Many Christians believe that some of the gifts ceased operating after the death of the first apostles and the completion of the New Testament, that they were part of a special dispensation of gifts meant to jump-start the new church. Others embrace many more gifts as God's provision for the present-day church. Not everyone falls solidly into the "cessationist," "Pentecostal," or "charismatic" camps. Many (if not most) of us are unsure, a little suspicious of excesses, cautiously interested but not adamant either way. Some of us, following in the footsteps of evangelical giants such as A.J. Gordon, A.B. Simpson, Andrew Murray, R.A. Torrey, and Dwight L. Moody, have a well-developed appreciation for the need for the Holy Spirit's power, but less grasp of the specifics of spiritual giftedness.[10]

I myself am a longtime charismatic within a denominational church. I have become increasingly comfortable with a wide range of gifts. I do not believe that certain gifts ceased when the last of the twelve apostles died. In each of us, spiritual gifts are blended with each other and expressed differently depending on our personalities, talents, and circumstances. I want to use descriptive gift names that are as scriptural as possible and to try not to blur the lines between spiritual gifts and inborn talents or personality traits. At the same time, I respect others' points of view—and God's ability to use us wherever we are. I want women (men too!) to feel comfortable in discussing the subject of spiritual gifts.

Limp Not. Nervousness about certain gifts, which can become vehement defensiveness, has often had the effect of making the body of Christ walk with a "limp."

If part of the human body isn't used, it atrophies. Muscles shrink. The rest of the body suffers and has to compensate. Just as a Chinese woman with her feet bound in the traditional fashion couldn't run and jump, neither can the local church or denomination "run" if some gifts of the Spirit are bound. Likewise, if a gift—such as evangelism or healing—is overemphasized, there will be a similar imbalance.

> An enormous eye or a gigantic hand wouldn't be a body, but a monster. What we have is one body with many parts, each its proper size and in its proper place. No part is important on its own. Can you imagine Eye telling Hand, "Get lost; I don't need you"? Or, Head telling Foot, "You're fired; your job has been phased out"? As a matter of fact, in practice it works the other way—the "lower" the part, the more basic, and therefore necessary. You can live without an eye, for instance, but not without a stomach.... The way God designed our bodies is a model for understanding our lives together as a church: every part dependent on every other part, the parts we mention and the parts we don't, the parts we see and the parts we don't.
>
> 1 CORINTHIANS 12:21-26, THE MESSAGE

Each gift and each individual person are essential to the vitality of the body of Christ.

Abuses

Besides quibbling over gift validity, Christians can be fearful of gift abuses. The danger of abuse can come from several directions: misuse of spiritual power, pride, immaturity, ignorance, and counterfeit gifts.

Power and pride. Spiritual gifts can confer a greater or lesser degree of power on gift holders. Power can be dangerous. Power plus ever-present human pride ensure failure.

Pride makes us grasp at our gifts, using them to prove our worth. Insecure women and men can grasp at—or take aim at—particular gifts because to do so seems to prove personal worth. If their role puts them in any position of authority over others, even informally, pride-wielded power can damage the body of Christ.

For example, Jeannette, a gifted administrator, was hired by a church just big enough to support her part-time services. She had attended the church for a short time and was eager to apply herself to her new duties, one of which was to count the weekly donations, previously the duty of a volunteer church treasurer. Everyone was relieved to have a good "organizer" on the small church staff, and they praised her for her efficiency.

Before long, however, some church members began to receive unwelcome phone calls from their new administrator. She had been scrutinizing their giving patterns and had taken it upon herself to urge them to give more to the church. Adopting a bill-collector mentality, Jeannette wanted to achieve the goal of having a church where every member contributes a tithe. No more small change in the offering plate, brothers and sisters!

Overnight, the pastor was required to become a full-time peacemaker in his congregation. He tried to curb Jeannette's overzealous approach to her duties. Almost every day, he needed to soothe hot tempers. "She can't tell me how much to give! ... Who does she think she is?" Contributions dropped drastically. Even after noting that, pride prevented Jeannette from accepting correction; she was angry at everyone and felt betrayed. Originally hired to be an asset to the life of the congregation, she had become a detriment instead. Eventually, she was removed from her post in disgrace, and she moved to another church.

Immaturity. Sometimes it isn't so much a question of insecurity as it is incompleteness. Sometimes we are out of balance because we need more help from God's Spirit to come into our full inheritance as his children.

Here is a personal example. As I entered young adulthood, I began to discover that I had spiritual gifts that enabled me to pray with people one-on-one, to their benefit. Every time I helped someone in this way, I gloried in the afterglow. I loved to remember how it felt to have so much of God's pure love flowing through me to another person. I would "wear out" each recollection. Gradually, however, I began to wake up to the fact that this might be unhealthy. I began to see how the devil could sideswipe me, taking advantage of the fact that my eyes of faith were not fixed on God the Rock but instead on rewarding recollections of successes. Over the course of a year, I regularly prayed, "Lord, make me able to love you more than I love your works." I became increasingly sure that I had never had a "first love" for Jesus. So I prayed for that too.

Months later, I was at a women's retreat where I had an opportunity to receive prayer. Stubbornly, I decided that I was not going to leave that place until I received what I had been requesting for so long. My stubbornness must have reflected God's sovereign timing, because when I mentioned my need, the woman who was ready to pray for me simply repeated my request: "Lord, make Kathy love you more than your works," and my whole orientation changed in one moment.

Talk about answered prayer! I have never been the same since. I began to love Jesus with a passion I never had thought possible, and my use of spiritual gifts took second place to that.

Counterfeit gifts. False gifts do exist, counterfeits of either human or satanic origin. New Age influences and other beliefs based on non-Christian religions, some of which include a heavy emphasis on the supernatural, cause confusion about spiritual gifts.

Not every supernatural-seeming gift is from the Holy Spirit. Pharaoh's wizards could work genuine miracles that imitated God's wonders. Were they supernatural? Yes. Were they of God? No. The telephone psychic may predict your future accurately. Is she a prophet of God? See Deuteronomy 18:9-14. Counterfeits do imitate the real thing. Let's not be afraid of the real thing just because it has been imitated.

People can speak in tongues because they are under the influence of an evil power or because they are psychologically disturbed. The following example has occurred in some form in many places.

A new Christian, eighteen-year-old Amy was a shy freshman at a small Christian college. The housing office had placed her with three suitemates. Eager to make new friends, she joined the girls' informal prayer group. One of them told Amy, "You need to be baptized in the Holy Spirit if you want to be a 'real Christian.'" Amy agreed compliantly, and they laid hands on her and prayed over her. The other girls prayed partly in English and partly in what sounded like foreign languages to Amy. "Now you must speak in tongues!" the oldest girl insisted. They all prayed louder while Amy grew red. Surely her first week of school wouldn't end with her new friends thinking she wasn't even a Christian! It almost did, because Amy couldn't make a sound.

After talking about it constantly, the girls more or less told her that if she didn't get the gift of tongues, they didn't want her for a roommate. Amy was distraught. She didn't know what to do. The situation occupied her mind every moment. Eventually, she asked for prayer again, this time speaking out in a gibberish she had invented so they would think more highly of her. It worked; her suitemates accepted her.

In Amy's case, her "gift of tongues" was a psychological response based on fear. She ended up receiving some counseling and now understands why she faked it, but Amy has been deeply suspicious of the validity of spiritual gifts ever since.

Seek the Giver and the Gifts

In spite of abuses, spiritual gifts have continued to appear throughout church history. The church today faces extreme challenges as did the early church. God's provision throughout the centuries has been the same: spiritual equipment for the saints (that includes you and me!). A vital part of the spiritual equipment of the body of Christ is spiritual giftedness.

Our spiritual gifts, designed to equip us to take our places of service and ministry in the local and universal body of Christ, will help to usher in the rule of the kingdom of God on earth. The gifts are not for our personal ego satisfaction or so that we can become successful or prominent. Neither can we peer at our gifts under a spiritual microscope, anymore than we can capture the wind. We are encouraged to desire the spiritual gifts (see 1 Cor 14:1) but we can't demand certain ones; they have been assigned to us by God. Although we can keep them whether we use them well or misuse them, we can't store our gifts in their gift boxes or any other kind of boxes.

Therefore, without dictating the results to our heavenly Father, let's use the free gifts we have received. Let's become spiritually liberated women who are free to use our gifts for God's glory, excited to see the results. Our God is an awesome God! He created us to know him, never cutting us off when we are confused. If we focus on him, he will always guide us.

> God helping you: Take your everyday, ordinary life—your sleeping, eating, going-to-work, and walking-around life—and place it before God as an offering. Embracing what God does for you is the best thing you can do for him.
>
> ROMANS 12:1, THE MESSAGE

Michael Harper, respected British expert on spiritual gifts, writes, "It used to be said that we should seek 'the Giver, not the gifts,' That is only half true. A better statement is, 'the Giver and the gifts.'" [11]

Three

Spiritual Gifts and You

Jill MacGregor is a Supermom in the best sense of the word. She's a real person and that's her real name. As I write this, she is pregnant with her fourth child. Her other children, three girls, are ages three, four, and eight. A Christian since age fourteen, Jill's a native Floridian, surrounded by a large extended family. She is happily married to her husband, Travis, with whom she shares some unique interests such as raising wild hogs and competing in sprint triathalons (before they had children).

Besides her energetic life as a wife, home-schooling mother, and athlete, Jill manages to find the time for creative writing. She's a published and awarded author who writes short stories, essays, Bible-school curricula, children's literature, song lyrics, plays, musicals, and poetry.

More on Jill later. Now look at a woman I'll call Debbie. Debbie is not a Supermom by anybody's definition. She and I were neighbors when my children were small. She would lament, "I am the most ungifted woman I know! I can't keep house, can't cook a decent meal, can't sew. I can't even peel an apple. I can't sing or play a musical instrument. My handwriting is awful and my spelling is worse. Sometimes I can be a bit humorous, but only by accident. My head is off in the clouds somewhere—I can't remember whether or not I went to my

Bible study last week. I worry too much. I'm scared to drive on the expressway. About all I can do 'well' is to yell at my kids—my mothering skills are so bad too. No talents, no abilities ... I don't even think I have any reliable *instincts!*"

Even though we probably would rank ourselves somewhere between the Jills and the Debbies of the world, most of us can identify with their struggles to comprehend the subject of giftedness. We may be familiar with Debbie's lament: "No gifts, not me! I got left out in the distribution, shortchanged." If we consider the subject at all (many women just don't), we may also be aware of some of Jill's puzzlements: "I've been blessed with many interests and talents, but what's the dividing line between a natural ability and a spiritual gift? How does God want me to view my giftedness? Are natural talents sometimes the same as spiritual gifts?"

Let's look at that last question first.

Natural Versus Spiritual Gifts

Our spiritual gifts, imparted to us upon our conversion, are not the same as the "talent packages" we were born with. At the same time, the talents and abilities with which we were born are part of our Creator's gifting for our lives. God distributes talents and abilities across the board to every human being alive. His distribution system may not seem "fair," but it certainly reflects his sweeping, creative lordship.

Both natural talents and spiritual gifts tend to integrate other people into our lives. For instance, if writing is your natural gift, you do need a reader or two to feel fulfilled. If you have a talent for talking, you need at least one listener. (That person should be sure to nod and smile every now and then.) If you also have the spiritual gift of teaching, you need some listeners (or readers) to teach. If your talent is baking, you need someone to lick that bowl and polish off that plate of cookies. If you also have a spiritual gift of hospitality, you need someone to serve.

We notice that many of our natural abilities have been inherited from our parents. Some are obvious: musical or artistic ability, mechanical ability, a "mind for math," a "way with words." Others are more subtle but worth appreciating.

One of the natural qualities my mother possessed was a sense of *adventure*. Capable of finding the most interesting aspect of any situation, she rose to the challenge of a crisis by finding the intrigue or the humor of the moment. With her, even running out of gas in the middle of nowhere could become an adventure. Her natural curiosity also taught me to look things up, a trait that drives my four kids nuts when some arcane subject comes up at the dinner table and I run for the encyclopedia. These traits are not the same as my spiritual gifts, however, which have been "inherited," if you will, directly from God.

John Wesley, eighteenth-century father of the Methodist church, distinguished between *ordinary gifts* (which he defined as talents and moral virtues) and *extraordinary gifts of the Holy Spirit* (i.e., spiritual gifts, although Wesley didn't define them further).[1] Another term applied to ordinary, inborn gifts is "common grace." We've all got common grace.

Upon our conversion to Christianity, our natural, "common grace" gifts should be dedicated to the service of Jesus Christ. This doesn't always occur, mostly through innocent ignorance on our part. We need to cooperate with the Holy Spirit as he helps bring out the full potential of our inborn gifts.

Spiritual gifts may parallel consecrated natural talents. They are "super-added" to natural gifts, often so interwoven with them "that it demands quite an effort of clear thinking to keep them distinct in our minds."[2] Like natural gifts, they can be developed or not by a combination of God's help and our willingness.

"Converted" Talents? This doesn't mean that our talents translate directly into spiritual gifts. Bruce Bugbee, founder and president of Network Ministries and author of *What You Do Best in the Body of Christ,* writes, "After personally leading over twelve thousand people through this [gift-] discovery process, I have not been able to identify when, and for whom, a natural talent will be equivalent to a spiritual gift." Bugbee says he sees it sometimes, such as a nurse with a gift of mercy or a salesman with the gift of evangelism. On the other hand, he notes that being a good schoolteacher doesn't guarantee the spiritual gift of teaching, and being an effective manager in the secular workplace does not guarantee the gift of leadership or administration.[3]

Kenneth Cain Kinghorn writes in his book, *Gifts of the Spirit,* "Spiritual gifts function as incarnations of God's power in human life. Sometimes they flow through and heighten our natural abilities, and sometimes they work independently of personal aptitudes. In any case, spiritual gifts complement and blend with our humanity."[4]

Getting It Straight

Our human abilities and talents were not designed to enable us to perform spiritual tasks. The apostle Paul writes that his natural talents were *not* considerable (see 2 Cor 10:10). Yet what a spiritual powerhouse he was!

Spiritual gifts, given by God to everyone who has given his or her life to Jesus Christ, are designed specifically to foster spiritual growth and Christian service. Some spiritual gifts are flashier than others. Nevertheless, even the most hidden ones point to God as the source.

> Now there are varieties of gifts, but the same Spirit; and there are varieties of service, but the same Lord; and there are varieties of working, but it is the same God who inspires them all in every one. To each is given the manifestation of the Spirit for the common good.
>
> 1 CORINTHIANS 12:4-7, RSV

The purpose of spiritual gifts is to help build the body of Christ on earth. Jesus' Spirit, dwelling in the hearts of believers, brings his very character to the world.

"Moonlight dries no mittens." I love this line from poet Carl Sandburg. It reminds me that we need the sun (Son) to "dry our mittens"; we need him in order to do our spiritual assignments. How helpful it is to learn to distinguish the difference between natural abilities and spiritual gifts, both so we can get into the flow of God's Spirit for our own lives and so we can receive the benefits of others' spiritual gifts!

Debbie can relax, knowing that although her inborn talents seem to be very limited, she is useful in the kingdom of God because she is guaranteed to have been given spiritual gifts. Jill can relax too, not spending her energy developing one of her talents for its own sake, but submitting everything to her Lord and Savior. What a relief to know that our job is to become more responsive to the Lord of our lives, not more responsible for our own lives.

Great and terrible day. Without the gifts of the Spirit, the church is not the body of Christ on earth, but one more human organization. A.W. Tozer emphasized that it's vital to get these natural/spiritual distinctives straight. In *Tragedy in the Church: the Missing Gifts,* he writes,

> A Christian congregation can survive and often appear to prosper in the community by the exercise of human talent and without any touch from the Holy Spirit. All that religious activity and the dear people will not know anything better until the great and terrible day when our self-employed talents are burned with fire and only that which was wrought by the Holy Ghost will stand forever.[5]

I, for one, want to be working in concert with my Lord, so that on that day I will have something to show for my lifelong journey.

Gifts for Each and Every One

The point needs to be repeated: *If you are a believer, the Holy Spirit has given you spiritual gifts.* Yes, you. No exceptions.

"We have different gifts, according to the grace given us" (Rom 12:6a). Did you catch that? "*We* [that includes you, includes Debbie] *have* [without a doubt] different gifts...."

From Paul's first letter to the Corinthians: "Now to each one the manifestation of the Spirit is given for the common good" (1 Cor 12:7). There's no uncertainty here, either. It's a stated fact: "To *each one ... is given....*"

Peter exhorted believers similarly: "As each has received a gift, employ it for one another, as good stewards of God's varied grace" (1 Pt 4:10, RSV).

He gave you gifts when you were born into his family and became his beloved child. He gave you gifts—to change the birthday analogy just a little—to equip you for your kingdom role, very much as bridal-shower gifts equip the bride for her new role.

Gifted to be the Lord's bride, you step into the "brideship" of the worldwide body of believers. The church itself is seen as a bride. In metaphorical terms, *her* love, *her* mission, *her* response comprise a feminine response. All the parts of the body are working toward the goal of perfect brideship; receptive and full of courage born of loving obedience to the Bridegroom (see Eph 5:24-27, 32; Rv 21:9-10).

You are a very original piece of work. From your beginnings in the mind of God (see Ps 139:13-18; Jer 1:5a), your Creator has endowed you with your own particular blend of personality traits, natural gifts, and spiritual gifts. You can't exchange these gifts at some celestial department store, nor should you want to. Instead, refer to the Manufacturer's instructions to discover the full potential of each one.

Saved to serve. A bride's new role is a role of service to her husband and future family. Spiritual "shower" gifts equip each of us to serve Jesus' purposes in the family of God.

Leslie Flynn, author of the spiritual gifts classic, *19 Gifts of the Spirit,* tells us, "God would have taken us to heaven immediately at conversion had He no purpose for us here. Among other purposes, 'we are saved to serve.' To equip for service, God gives one or more spiritual gifts to every child of His."[6]

Veteran spiritual-gifts teacher C. Peter Wagner expresses it well:

> I realize that it comes as a surprise to some Christians, who have been only marginally active in church for years, to find

> out that they are needed, wanted and gifted to do their part in their local church.... No substitute exists for finding your gift-mix and knowing for sure that you are equipped to do just what God designed you to do.[7]

Texas pastor and author Rick Godwin says that if two of us in a church have exactly the same gifts, one of us is superfluous. You are entirely unique and necessary to the body of Christ.

Sure, you may be a "work in progress." Who isn't? If you are letting your Master work on you, you are in the best hands of all. I hope you have already discovered that you are only free to be your original self when you let the Holy Spirit encompass your weaknesses and liberate your gifts.

No matter how imperfect you are, you have ideal qualifications for your kingdom assignment if you put yourself at divine disposal. You are in good company. From the original apostles on down through church history, awareness of one's own inadequacy and corresponding awareness of dependence upon God is vital.

As we learn to rely as much as possible on our Savior, we become our true selves. Insignificant events become significant. Whether or not you ever move mountains by a monumental gift of faith, you will find joy and fulfillment in something as simple as helping to fold church bulletins. Step into your inheritance. You have been given particular gifts. Find out more about them so you can live the life you were created to live!

Free Gifts

Gifts are given to each of us by God's generous grace, not according to our supposed merit. The very word *gifts* (Greek: *charismata*) has as its root word *charis* ("grace").

No gift is singled out as a sign of special heavenly approval. In fact, Paul compares the gifts to the parts of the human body, some of which are on public view and some of which are kept hidden (see 1 Cor 12:12-25). The body is not complete without all of its parts, even the less presentable ones. "But to each one of us grace has been given as Christ apportioned it" (Eph 4:7).

The gifts have been assigned to believers "according to his will" (Heb 2:4), not as spiritual merit badges you can earn. If you feel cheated in the distribution, you should ask for God's help to appreciate what he has given you. He loves you too much to have shortchanged you.

And a woman who has a particularly strong gift does not have a guarantee of spiritual maturity. We all know men and women who have used their spiritual gifts in distressingly immature ways. If we were God, we might decide to withdraw the gifts from those who abuse them. Not God—as the Giver of all good gifts, he lets you keep them whether you use them responsibly or not. He won't revoke your gifts (see Rom 11:29).

For your part, you need to remember that you didn't give yourself these gifts, nor can you use them well without God's ongoing assistance. So boasting is out (see 1 Cor 12:21-25). So is complaining (see 1 Cor 12:14-18). Either response betrays an immaturity and insecurity that the Lord can remedy, if we let him.

In addition, "navel gazing" is out. Don't talk about a gift too much, sort of fondling it as you would a favorite puppy. Offer it back to God in willing service and you will discover more about the gift itself than you will by hugging it too closely.

We are *partners* with God's Spirit. He gives us gifts, one and all, and he knows what he is doing. In giving each of us gifts, with full foreknowledge that we will regularly mess things up, he nevertheless sticks to his plan. Ideally, we will recognize that we are accountable to him, that our gifts are not loaned to us or, worse, leased to us. Realizing that "God don't make no junk," we will be grateful and humble, and eager to say, "Here I am; send me!"

Body Life

If I were running a universe, I would use my omnipotence to take care of all the details instead of handing them over to underlings who are guaranteed to be unreliable. Apparently, God doesn't think that way. God seems to take a lot of risks with human beings. He invests his whole self in us.

"We are members of his body" (Eph 5:30). According to some early manuscripts, Paul's choice of words in his letter to the Ephesians indicates that we are like "bone of his bone and flesh of his flesh." Think of it! When you exercise any spiritual gift, Jesus Christ himself is at work through you.

When Jesus was on earth, he was limited to the range of his earthly body.

> He was one man, walking beside one sea in one little corner of the earth. He healed whomever He touched, but His touch was necessarily limited by time and space.... We are to complete His mission. We are His multiplied hands, His feet,

His voice and compassionate heart. Imperfect and partial to be sure, but His healing Body just the same.[9]

Now, because his present body, the church, is almost everywhere on the planet, Jesus has practically unlimited range. You and I are part of that body. Our gifts, put together with the gifts of every believer, enable the body of Christ to have replenished life and to do Christ's work all over the earth, year after year after year.

Yet so often we are neutralized in our effectiveness. Neglect of and ignorance about the spiritual gifts with which we are equipped has greatly hampered Jesus' ability to reach out in the power of his Holy Spirit through us.

Needing each other. Jesus himself has all the spiritual gifts. No other individual ever has or ever will. However, when we are pulled together in the worldwide church, we demonstrate all the gifts in action.

This opens new possibilities for the meaning of Jesus' words to his disciples, "Truly, truly, I say to you, he who believes in me will also do the works that I do; and greater works than these will he do, because I go to the Father" (Jn 14:12, RSV). As an individual, I've never done a "greater work" than Jesus himself did 2000 years ago, but I am part of a seamless continuation of his work by the activity of the Holy Spirit through the centuries.

In Paul's letter to the Romans, his first letter to the Corinthians, and his letter to the Ephesians (see Rom 12; 1 Cor 12; Eph 4), he explains spiritual gifts in the context of the body of Christ. The gifts are to equip us to take our places in the local and universal body of Christ in service and ministry, to ensure that the rule of the kingdom of God spreads. They are "to equip the saints for the work of ministry, for building up the body of

Christ" (Eph 4:12, RSV). Christians are called to serve, not to be served.

This is not a difficult concept to grasp, especially for women. We already know we need other people. We already know we can't stand alone. (It usually doesn't take us very long to figure this out.) We just need to expand this idea to realize that our spiritual gifts can't stand alone either. No one person is gifted enough, wise enough, or strong enough to do God's work alone. Our gifts will die if unsupported by the gifts of others in the body of Christ. We truly need each other.

This point is often emphasized in church newsletters and elsewhere by the following anonymous illustration:

> Xvxn though my typxwritxr is an old modxl, it works wxll xnough xxcxpt for onx of its kxys. I havx wishxd many timxs that it workxd pxrfxctly. It is trux that thxrx arx 45 kxys that function, but just onx kxy makxs all the diffxrxncx. So thx nxxt timx you think you arx only onx pxrson and that your xffort is not nxxdxd, rxmxmbxr my typxwritxr and say to yoursxlf, "I am a kxy pxrson. Thx Lord nxxds mx."

Go for it! Even from your spiritual babyhood, you are a useful member of Christ's body. Everywhere he traveled, the apostle Paul started new churches. All he had to work with were baby Christians. Within a short time after the establishment of each local church, believers had grown in the use of enough different gifts to make for commentary (see 1 Cor 14).

Paul himself was commissioned to serve God in spiritual giftedness immediately upon his conversion. A believer named Ananias (who must have been quaking in his sandals as he obeyed the Spirit's urging to speak with such a dangerous man—exercising his gift of prophecy, by the way), told Paul, "'The God of our fathers appointed you to know his will, to see the Just One and to hear a voice from his mouth; for you will be a witness for him to all men of what you have seen and heard" (Acts 22:14-15, RSV).

Why would God select such a violent man, one who had hated the name of Jesus of Nazareth, to carry the Good News far and wide? We know now, of course, that God knew what he was doing! Should we be so surprised when this same God calls each of us by name and situates us in the church, equipping us with "every good gift"?

If you currently feel like a square peg in a round hole, maybe you're not using your spiritual gifts to maximum advantage. When you begin to concentrate on using the tools you have been given, you'll just slide into that hole as if you were made for it ... because you *were*. "For we are God's workmanship, created in Christ Jesus to do good works, which God prepared in advance for us to do" (Eph 2:10). Should we be so surprised that whatever our Creator gives us to do seems like such a perfect fit?

When you discover and use your spiritual gifts, you feel you are doing and being what you were originally created to do and be. You may be stretched and challenged, but you will do your particular assignment well because you have the gifts with which to do it. Doing a good job leads to personal fulfillment and a sense of belonging and purpose.

Perhaps you feel like Debbie, still not convinced that you have any spiritual gifts at all, at least not very obvious ones. Or maybe you are, like Jill, sometimes wondering about how your natural talents and spiritual gifts blend together. You get the picture, but it's still fuzzy.

That's OK. This is just a beginning. Read on to meet more women who are discovering their spiritual gifts.

Four

Unburied Treasure

Early in her Christian life, Ellen had noticed that other girls often came to her for advice. "It was kind of a pain, really," she told her small Bible-study group. "In high school, I would be trying to do my homework and I would be interrupted all the time by my friends—especially when they were stressed out. I would listen to their problems, and then I would tell them what occurred to me. Somehow, I seemed to be able to put into words the help they needed."

The pattern had continued into adulthood. Ellen's common-sense wisdom seemed to advertise itself wherever she went. She didn't exactly give advice; it was more like *perspective.* In fact, if someone would say, "Ellen, I need your advice," Ellen would not be one of those people who would give her Steps One through Ten. She just listened quietly and then offered some pertinent observation that had come from her own somewhat-difficult life. Others appreciated her stabilizing influence and told her they respected her for it. After she began to realize that God had given her the spiritual gift of wisdom, she became even more generous with it.

Ellen's friend Valerie also had the gift of wisdom, although her circumstances were more restricted. Valerie was married to a well-known television newscaster. Everywhere she went, people recognized her name. She had learned to be very careful about what she said, so it wouldn't be reported somewhere out of context. Others respected her for her wise restraint. She was intensely aggravated sometimes by the personal limitations of her semipublic role, but she could share her deepest heart with certain close friends, such as Ellen. The women in the Bible study loved her. Mostly, she used her wisdom to benefit her husband and two teenage children. She was a good illustration of the adage, "Behind every great man is a great woman."

Patty was always trying to find the secret of success. Joining the Bible study was part of her search for true friendship, which had always eluded her. "I want to get my needs met" was her unspoken motto. Patty admired both Ellen and Valerie. As the weeks went by, she unconsciously began to imitate her new friends in an effort to obtain people's respect. She had collected plenty of advice over the years, some of it good and some of it bad, so she began to parrot wise-sounding phrases she had heard before. She even bought a pair of glasses similar to Ellen's in an effort to look more intellectual. However, the respect she craved eluded her. In her effort to find favor, she never noticed the spiritual gifts she did have, such as the gift of mercy.

Another woman in the Bible study shared a heartrending prayer request. Ellen and Valerie listened. With their quiet wisdom, they seemed to be able to pray easily. Ellen added a few helpful words after the group prayer. Patty had wanted to *cry* instead of pray, but that just had seemed so out of place. "The others will think that I'm just a glob of emotional jelly!" she had churned inside. "I must stop the tears and say something intelligent!"

Because she had compared herself so unfavorably to others, Patty never discovered the gift of mercy that her merciful God had planted within her. If only she had realized that the gift of mercy was like buried treasure inside her. She had burdened her friends with a facsimile of someone else instead of becoming true to herself in Christ. God had made Patty just as special as he had made Ellen and Valerie. Valerie and Ellen had seen their gifts grow as they had invested them in others. Patty had, in effect, buried her gift.

Do Ellen, Valerie, and Patty have something in common with the servants in Jesus' parable of the talents (see Mt 25:14-28; Lk 19:12-26)? Perhaps we can see ourselves in them. Are you an Ellen or a Valerie, a faithful servant growing in confidence as you share your gifts with others? Or are you a Patty, actually gifted but feeling shortchanged and afraid to invest your gift? The faithful Ellens of the world are not sinless (no one is), but they are at God's disposal, using their energy to share God's love through their gifts. Their Master commends them for investing so wisely.

We must do something with the gifts we have been given. If we don't, perhaps because of confusion or fear, we are like the unworthy servant who buried his money in the ground where it could neither grow nor do anyone any good. We don't exactly *lose* the gift, but it might just as well be lost if it remains buried.

What might be causing us to bury some of our gifts?

Confusion. Patty didn't understand that she was the possessor of a gift that was equally valuable—but very different—from the gifts of her wise friends Ellen and Valerie. She was confused and ashamed of herself for her tears, because Ellen and Valerie almost never cried.

In fact, Patty's tears were one of her signals that her gift of mercy was in gear. She didn't need to have wise words on her lips; often others didn't want more advice. Her gift equipped her to be a compassionate *listener*, to "weep with those who weep."

Her confusion about her gifts was not helped by her self-centered approach to relationships. Perhaps if she had begun to ask God to help her reach out to others, she would have begun to understand who God made her to be.

Fear. The unworthy servant was afraid of his master's harsh opinion. Are we sometimes afraid of the opinions of others?

A Christian bank employee left her Bible in plain sight on her desk as a silent witness to her faith. Occasionally, a customer remarked about it, but no one had ever complained about it. One day, a bank officer saw it. "Never leave your Bible out again!" he commanded angrily. Now she was terrified that she would lose her job if she even wore her cross necklace to work. If the bank employee had any gifts that would have motivated her to share her faith, they are now buried under her timidity.

By contrast, a Christian schoolteacher was reprimanded for explaining the meaning of Christmas in her public-school class. The rebuke didn't seem reasonable to her, but she complied—for that year anyway. As the next holiday season approached, she developed a creative strategy. She asked a Christian mother of one of her pupils to come in and give an engaging "How Our Family Celebrates Christmas" presentation, complete with a show-and-tell crèche and little gingerbread cookies. The teacher wouldn't let her strong gift of evangelism be buried under a layer of school protocol. The class, which included some immigrant children from Saudi Arabia, interacted freely with the visiting mom, saying, "I didn't know all this! I thought Christmas was just Santa Claus and gifts like I see on TV."

I once heard about a woman who was a lifelong missionary to India. She was blessed with many spiritual gifts, notably as a missionary and for voluntary poverty. She could preach and teach. She could organize and administer. She could hear God's voice. A multifaceted medical mission developed under her gifted leadership. Once, when medicines were scarce, intractible illnesses were cured through her prayers. But that scared her. Afraid of having her mission become a kind of sideshow, she pleaded, "Take it back, Lord!" and she never prayed for healing again. Her fear had buried her gift of healing.

Dig It Up

Potential martyrs have repudiated their faith to save their skins. Christian teachers have missed their calling. Evangelists have wasted a lifetime netting fish (or cleaning house or fishing for compliments) instead of winning fellow human beings in need of salvation. We've all missed the boat to some extent, whether because of fear, confusion, or our inherent sinfulness.

It's a good thing that our Father's love for us is not based on our performance. Those of us who bury our gifts are no less loved by God than those who have invested them in others from day one. But if we were "saved to serve," we should be tripping all over ourselves in our eagerness to serve our Savior with the gifts with which he has equipped us. We have the very power of God within us.

Of course it does mean lots of work. Are we afraid sometimes that we will be asked to do more work than we can handle? God will never ask us to use our gifts without equipping us with strengthening grace—you can count on that. And you can expect your work to bear fruit. If you invest your gifts wisely as the Lord leads you, your investment will *multiply.* Guaranteed results! Reread the parable of the talents (see Mt 25:14-28; Lk 19:12-26).

If you dig up your buried gifts and begin to use them, you

can also count on a lifetime of *fulfillment*. Part of the "strengthening grace" that will help you work hard is the overflowing joy of doing what your Savior created you to do.

"I was *created* to do this!" Beverly enthused as she arranged figures on her flannel board. "When I joined this church, I volunteered to help with the coffee hour. Then I worked in the church office for a while. When my children were teenagers, I also served as a hostess and chaperone for their youth group activities. When the pastor asked me to teach the four-year-olds, it almost seemed like a demotion. But as soon as I began, I knew I had 'come home.' I love it! I've been doing it now for ten years. Even thinking about it gives me energy!"

Clean it off. Remember that gifts don't come in boxes. If one of your gifts has been buried in your spiritual backyard, it will be dirty. Though you will recognize it as your own, it may take time to learn how to operate it.

What if your "buried treasure" turns out to be kind of a dud? You were expecting a silver spoon and you got an old garden trowel. What do you do?

Ask your Manufacturer for instructions. He made you and he made the gift. You will be delighted to discover that your gifts have been perfectly fitted to your personality and even to your circumstances. You may need to wait a while to find out how that old trowel is meant to be used, but you will be so glad it's a trowel and not a silver demitasse spoon when you get sent out to work in the garden.

Pots and pans. When my husband and I got married, someone gave us an oversized cast-iron frying pan as a wedding gift. Cooking for just the two of us, I didn't need such a big pan. But I kept it. Over time, I accumulated more pans, mostly smaller ones. Some were quite specialized, such as my hinged-in-the-middle omelet pan. I had a medium-size stainless steel pan with a lid and a little one with nonstick coating. My collection of pans nested together on top of the granddaddy cast-iron pan, which became dusty with lack of use.

My family grew. Suddenly the cast-iron pan became quite useful. Now I need all my pans. I use them so much that none of them gets dusty. Someday, I will be cooking for two again. (I hope I remember how!) My cast-iron pan will probably remain in my cupboard until my grandchildren come for breakfast—and I'll be ready for them!

Our spiritual gifts are like kitchen pans. They are tools, divine equipment. Sometimes they just sit there for a long time because they're not needed. Sometimes they are used individually, but usually they are used with another gift. (What would my frying pan be without my spatula?)

Occasionally, we may need to "borrow" our neighbor's gift, just as I have always had to borrow a springform pan from my neighbor Barb. (My full array of frying pans doesn't help me when I want to make a cheesecake; I am deficient in springform pans.) We won't have all the gifts ourselves.

The same type of gift may come in granddaddy size or in petite, in cast iron or stainless steel or fine copper. As an evangelist, for instance, I may preach to thousands like Billy Graham, or I may have a very specialized niche in which the gift shines.

In my own life, I never would have thought I had a gift of evangelism. As far as I knew, I had never introduced anyone to Jesus as Savior except my own children. Then a few years ago I became acquainted with a few women from other countries who were working as researchers at the university in my city. I am not a scientist or a mathematician, and I can't speak Russian, Romanian, or Bulgarian—but we really "clicked." Through our warm friendship, several of them have become committed Christians. I have been able to present the gospel clearly and compellingly to my international friends—although nowhere else, to date. Do I have a specialized gift of evangelism? Maybe so, to judge by the results and by my enthusiasm. What a delightful surprise!

"Earnestly desire the spiritual gifts" (1 Cor 14:1b, RSV). Eugene Peterson paraphrases this as: "Give yourselves to the gifts God gives you" (THE MESSAGE).

Let's do it!

God's Blender

By now, three things should be clear: (1) all Christians possess spiritual gifts, (2) those spiritual gifts come in an infinite variety of expressions, and (3) if we use our spiritual gifts, we become fruitful Christians. *Variety* should be a key word as we prayerfully evaluate our own giftedness and learn to appreciate the way that spiritual gifts operate in others.

To more fully express God's love to the world around us, we need each others' gifts in all their splendid, blended specialization. "We have different gifts, according to the grace given us" (Rom 12:6a). Consider the relative strength of certain gifts in the Christians you know, the various applications of those gifts as they are blended with personality traits, other gifts, and level of maturity. A strong measure of our Christian maturity is the ability to appreciate each other in all our diversity.

Each of us needs to be put into God's blender. At the same time, we need to be blended together as a body of people.

A pinch of this, a dab of that. Everyone has enough of some gift to assume a role in the church. Think of all the behind-the-scenes tasks that need to be accomplished: Straightening the hymnals, trimming the bushes, cleaning the bathrooms, ordering the Easter lilies....

Our spiritual gifts also find an outlet in family life and in the working world. The woman with the gift of hospitality may be quick to volunteer to plan the office Christmas party or summer picnic. Every mother exercises a degree of the gift of administration as she organizes her family's day-to-day life. With or without a strong gift of teaching, we teach our children every day.

Sometimes what seems to be a weak gift early in life may blossom later in life. Conversely, what seems to be a new Christian's predominant gift may recede into the background as she moves through the years.

One-note bands. It is so easy for church leaders to give preference to certain gifts over others. Bodies of believers have certain corporate strengths, just as individual Christians do. One church may (often because of the gifts of its leaders) emphasize evangelism, teaching, healing, or mercy. There's nothing wrong with that if the congregation is encouraged to support the corporate calling with their full range of spiritual gifts. The difficulty comes when too many gifts are labelled as invalid and dropped out of the mix.

If a church begins to trumpet one note only—"Be saved!"—the average churchgoer may hear, "Become an evangelist or you're a loser." In a way, soul-winning evangelism may become an object of worship, and those in that church who lack the gift of evangelism may not realize their worth.

Across town, another church may be obsessed with feeding

the poor, refurbishing low-cost housing, and other acts of mercy. True as they are, Jesus' statement "Whatever you did for one of the least of these brothers of mine, you did for me" (Mt 25:40) becomes the only truth expounded upon from the pulpit. Compassion may predominate and a certain level of justice may be achieved—but absolutely no one is brought into the kingdom of God.

Meantime, in both congregations there are men and women and children whose hearts ache to do what they were created to do. They may even chastise themselves for their "waywardness" in straying from the party line. Some may earnestly but futilely strive to be effective evangelists or selfless dispensers of aid, all the while not realizing that their contributions should flow from their God-given gifts. Some may find a way to "bloom where they are planted." Many will not.

Those who do may well go unsung. The woman whose primary gift is helps may never, ever share the Four Spiritual Laws with another person. Behind the scenes, however, she may be the one person in the church who notices the neighborbood children hanging around the church playground, who befriends a few at a time and, with their parents' permission, brings them to Sunday school every week so that they can hear the Good News.

The elderly widow who faithfully rises in the wee hours of the morning to labor secretly in intercession may be the congregation's "secret weapon."

The single mom whose most notable feature is the dark circles under her eyes may be finding quiet joy in her annual efforts as the administrator of the vacation Bible school.

Each of us finds our meaning and function as a part of his body. But as a chopped-off finger or cut-off toe we wouldn't amount to much, would we? So since we find ourselves fashioned into all these excellently formed and marvelously functioning parts in Christ's body, let's just go ahead and be what we were made to be, without enviously or pridefully comparing ourselves with each other, or trying to be something we aren't.

ROMANS 12:5-6a, THE MESSAGE

Five

Life Bearers

Grandma Lucy lived in a trailer park where the climate was hot and humid most of the year. Her Social Security income was insufficient, and she was homebound because she had health problems and no car. To save money, she never used her air conditioning, even though her trailer often became fiercely uncomfortable on summer days.

Grandma Lucy was the oldest resident of the trailer park. Most of the other residents were young couples, most poorly educated, many unemployed, some married and some not. Between the roar of motorcycles, the loud music, and numerous verbal disputes, the park could be pretty unattractive and rough. The police came through regularly.

Lucy's home had faded to a pale turquoise hue, but her passion for Jesus had not faded. Lucy saw a need in her neighbors and felt called by God to meet it.

Always an early riser, she liked to use her oven before the hot sun came up. She decided to bake sweet things, especially her cinnamon rolls, and let the aroma drift out of her open windows. Passersby noticed the delectable fragrance of fresh-baked cinnamon rolls, so much more inviting than the smell of motor oil, garbage in the dumpsters, and exhaust fumes from the nearby highway. Lucy would keep her eye on the screen door and invite them in for a taste. Soon certain folks came every day.

A few kind words a day made a big difference for a lot of people.

They'd listen to her homespun wisdom—and look out for her well-being in return. ("Grandma Lucy! You better use that air conditioner today!") Along with her sticky buns and kind hospitality, she was dispensing God's love. They needed a grandma like her. For many young men and women, she became a welcome port in the storm. Over time and in a very natural way, she introduced her friends to the Anchor of her life, Jesus.

Womanly Grace

Grandma Lucy shows us something. Several things, actually, such as how to "bloom where you're planted" and how to let the fruit of the Holy Spirit (peace, love, gentleness; see Gal 5:22) make everything sweet. But I want to zero in on the special something that only women have—femininity.

Grandma Lucy's spiritual gifts of hospitality, giving, wisdom, and evangelism were infused with her nurturing nature and complemented by her womanly kitchen skills. Instinctively, she did what women do best: she was a life bearer.

Women bear other people's burdens well. The average woman will have a higher level of sympathy and compassion for those in need than the average man. Quick to roll up her sleeves to help, she nurtures her children or cares for elderly parents without being coerced. It's "just natural." And precisely because it's so ordinary, we fail to appreciate it.

Sometimes the compassionate touch of a woman can be the primary conveyance for the love of God. I'm thinking of Dorcee Clarey, who is a sixth-grade teacher in the Christian school my children attended. She is a dedicated teacher, easing one class after another over the hump into feisty adolescence.

She loves that age group, but the rigors of the job can be discouraging.

Once, she and I both happened to attend the same Christian conference. There was an opportunity to come forward for prayer for personal needs. Dorcee went forward. Drawn by a sense of her unknown need, I walked up right behind her and stood with my hands on her shoulders while prayers were being said. At one point I asked, "Is it OK if I stand so close behind you?" I noticed that she was crying as she nodded. Later, Dorcee told me it was the *touch* that meant so much. To her, I represented the other parents, and my supportive stance said to her, "I'm behind you 100 percent."

Women as Workers

Think of the large number of supportive roles in the church that would go unfilled if it weren't for women who volunteer their time. Why do we do it? Because someone twists our arms? Not usually.

We *want* to nurture those preschoolers, create those flower arrangements, cook those church suppers, design those banners, visit those shut-ins, lead that prayer group. Very often, we are expressing one of our spiritual gifts. Gifts look a little different in us than they do in men.

It's nothing new. In his first-century letter to Rome, Paul greets Mary, Tryphaena, Tryphosa, and Persis (see Rom 16:6, 12). "Everywhere that there was a church, women arose who worked doggedly.... No detail and no strenuous effort was too much or beneath them. In Rome, [these women] were among the stalwart women who served the church and seemed to breathe life into the very dust around them."[1]

Gifts Widespread in Women

Most women find that they possess one of the gifts listed below. However, any of the spiritual gifts, including any I have not mentioned below, are blended with femininity in distinct ways.

Helps, service, hospitality, mercy. Women are heavily represented in these areas of gifting. These gifts, undramatic and steady, are vital to the healthy functioning of a group of people. As mothers, mothers-in-law, friends, and neighbors, women illustrate the phrase that was used of the ancient Christians, "See how they love one another."

Many women are inclined to serve others in response to God's call to another person. For instance, to enable a young mother (who may have gifts of evangelism or as a missionary) to go on a short-term mission trip, friends may volunteer to baby-sit, cook meals, and do the family laundry while the mother is gone. Their hard work is just as vital to the advancement of God's kingdom as is that of the missionary.

Janice, a woman from New Jersey, takes young pregnant women who have chosen not to have abortions into her home. She offers welcome, structure, nurture, and unconditional love. Hospitality glows from the windows, and there is mercy even in times of conflict. Janice uses her gifts of hospitality and mercy every day.

Helps, service, hospitality, and mercy very often provide just the right "woman-friendly" starting place for women who are new to a church. Women often feel comfortable volunteering for some service project. Even a woman who lacks daytime flexibility may volunteer to sell tickets for a musical performance, make phone calls, cook a meal, or host a one-time event.

Shepherding/pastoring, exhortation, evangelism, teaching. Women often notice these gifts in the context of working with children. Especially to young children, the teacher is an extension of Mom. It doesn't matter so much if she's highly gifted in shepherding or teaching; what matters is tender expressions of care, and women have a corner on that. Sunday schools, founded in 1780 as a Christian outreach to uneducated street urchins, could never have existed and evolved for more than two hundred years without the multitudes of female teachers who have dedicated themselves to the task of teaching children about the gospel.

In one of her books, Edith Schaeffer writes about how she illustrated sermons for her restless children during long church services. With a pad of drawing paper, she combined her spiritual gifts of teaching and exhortation with her artistic talent. Her sketches were often simple stick figures with hearts for bodies. The children, snuggled close to her, loved those sermons.

Many women have possessed notable gifts of evangelism and teaching. Catherine Booth (1829–90), wife of William Booth, founder of the Salvation Army, is often considered to have been more gifted in evangelistic teaching (both spoken and written) than her better-known husband. Henrietta Mears (1890–1963) influenced generations of Christians through her years of teaching and evangelism at the First Presbyterian Church of Hollywood, California. Her classes in the 1940s included such students as Billy Graham, Bill Bright, and other now-prominent Christian leaders, and she became a cofounder of Gospel Light Publications.

Hospitality, already mentioned as a high feminine attribute, is closely allied with shepherding and teaching (see 1 Tm 3:2). For both gifts, *feed* is a key word. Women with these gifts want to take initiative to feed people both physically and spiritually.

Intercession, faith. We hear of churches in which a faithful widow prayed long, lonely years, and her prayers were heard. Women, especially in their older years when more energetic gifts may need to take a backseat, frequently become intercessors. Typically equipped with a greater gift of faith than they possessed before, they may be motivated by mercy to care for people in prayer. They may be motivated by prophecy, seeing God's plan and "praying into" it. Without such women, both young and old, faithful in their "prayer closets," the church would falter.

Pioneering missionary William Carey (1761–1834), worked for forty-one years in India in a time when Englishmen were not expected to survive more than six *months* in that country. One of his "secret weapons" was his paralyzed, bedridden sister in England, who prayed continuously for him. Her intercession accomplished far more than anyone can know.[2]

Leadership, wisdom, administration. More women are represented in these areas of gifting than will ever step forward to claim their giftedness. It often comes as a surprise to a woman to discover that she actually has such a spiritual gift—she just knows she enjoys overseeing the midweek daycare program or leading the Girl Scouts' annual camping expedition.

Roberta Hestenes, currently the senior pastor of Solana Beach Presbyterian Church in California, possesses the gift of leadership to such a degree that, during her nine-year tenure as president of Eastern College near Philadelphia, she became the founding director of the Roberta Hestenes Center for Christian Women in Leadership. Dr. Hestenes also possesses gifts of teaching (she was asked to teach communications at Fuller Theological Seminary before she had any advanced degrees) and served on the ministerial staffs of several

Presbyterian churches before becoming ordained.

Roberta may be exceptional, but Brenda is not. She had worked for years as an office manager. Her children were grown, and her husband, who was several years older than she, had just retired. She was deliberating whether to retire early herself or to keep working, perhaps in a less-demanding office, when her pastor offered her the new position of administrative secretary.

Brenda accepted the new job. She found that it used her spiritual gifts (primarily administration, wisdom, and mercy), her acquired office-managing skills, and her mature femininity better than any job she had ever had. The pastor often overcommitted his time or offended church members. Inobtrusively, Brenda was able to "be the mom" in the church office, smoothing over rough moments and helping the disorganized pastor meet his obligations with new efficiency and grace.

Women Together

Women often find special satisfaction in relating to other women—thus the large number of women's organizations both within the church and outside it. We gravitate to women's fellowship groups of all sorts, from neighborhood Bible studies to nationwide organizations such as Women's Aglow Fellowship International, MOPS (Mothers of Pre-Schoolers), Moms in Touch International, or Concerned Women for America. These fellowships attract women because, within them, women can express themselves in a way that may not have an outlet elsewhere. In some cases, because of theological or cultural standards, women-only groups may be the only context in which women with certain spiritual gifts can exercise them.

In the early church, although scholars dispute over details, the order of widows (later called deaconesses), based on Titus 2:3-4, seems to have been an official office for mature women. "Each male ministry had a sort of female counterpart, of a subordinate character and connected with the extension of [each] ministry to women."[3]

The proliferation of women's groups today carries on this tradition informally. Both for cultural reasons and for reasons of preference, women need other women.

Gifts of New Testament Women

Reread the New Testament in the light of women's spiritual gifts. Of course you will notice Dorcas (helps, giving) and Martha of Bethany (hospitality, service), but don't stop there. Take almost every woman you read about, and think about her probable gifts:

- Mary, mother of Jesus (faith, helps [Lk 1:38, Jn 2:3-5])
- Anna (intercession, prophecy [Lk 2:36-38])
- Elizabeth, mother of John the Baptist (prophecy [Lk 1:57-63])
- Phoebe (helps, probably other gifts [Rom 16:1-2])
- Priscilla (teaching, knowledge, wisdom, hospitality [Acts 18])
- Mary, John Mark's mother (hospitality [Acts 12:12])
- Apphia of Colossae (hospitality [Phlm 2])
- Mary Magdalene, Joanna, Susanna, and others who traveled with the disciples, supporting them "out of their own means" (helps, giving [Lk 8:2-3])
- Nearly anonymous "hard workers" such as Mary, Tryphaena, Tryphosa, and Persis (helps and possibly evangelism [Rom 16:6, 12])[4]

Pamela Smith, author of the book, *Woman Gifts,* writes,

"When we look back at the [New Testament] church, we find women leading and shaping as well as taking smaller steps. Lydia, Priscilla, and Chloe gather the church in their homes.... The daughters of Philip the evangelist are prophets. Phoebe is a deacon.... Rhoda answers the door."[5]

Gifts in Action Through the Centuries

Throughout church history, we find examples of women using their spiritual gifts. Most women remain nameless to us, but we do know about women in the early centuries of the church who founded religious communities. For example, Macrina the Younger (A.D. 328–380) worked in the Greek church with her brothers, Basil of Caesarea and Gregory Nazianzus. She founded and led a monastic house for women and reportedly exercised gifts of healing, prophecy, and teaching.[6] Many others have been canonized over the centuries by the Roman Catholic Church because of their notable spiritual achievements.

Courageous women have followed the leading of the Holy Spirit into sometimes hellish circumstances. In the prisons of England in the early 1800s, female inmates, along with their children, endured inhumane conditions. This attracted the attention of Elizabeth Fry (1780–1845), a Quaker woman with eleven children. She "spent countless hours inside prison bars—in spite of the many warnings she was given about the danger. She taught women how to sew and quilt and how better to care for themselves and their children. She read the Scriptures daily to inmates and obtained Bibles for those who wanted them.... Her efforts produced what seemed like a miracle: orderly disciplined inmates who became known for their work ethic."[7] Impelled by her gift of mercy, Elizabeth also helped the homeless and pioneered a nurses' school.

In Victorian England, motivated as much by her gift of evangelism as by mercy, Ellen Ranyard's Bible Mission (1857) employed working-class women as evangelists in London's slums.

During the Crimean War and afterward, Florence Nightingale (1820–1910), credited with founding modern-day medical nursing, followed God's leading to use her gifts of mercy and leadership despite family and societal disapproval. Although unconventional in her beliefs, she said, "There never was any vagueness in my plans or ideas as to what God's work was for me."[8]

More than one woman since Priscilla in the New Testament has been propelled into the public eye by her use of the gift of teaching, often combined with wisdom, exhortation, administration, leadership, and, some say, apostle. A small and varied sampling would include Italian Catherine of Siena (1347–80); French mystic Madame Jeanne Guyon (1648–1717); American colonist Anne Hutchinson (1591–1643); English Methodist Lady Selina Hastings (1707–91); New York "Mother of the Holiness Movement," Phoebe Palmer (1807–74); and the Philadelphia Quaker, author of *The Christian's Secret of a Happy Life* (1870), Hannah Whitall Smith. Every church tradition has a list of dauntless, gifted women who, to the present day, continue to contribute to the vitality of the church.

You and I can take inspiration from such women as we toil in relative obscurity. After all, the well-known women who have gone before us were only doing what came to hand, just as we are. The happy meshing of their giftedness and their circumstances was orchestrated by the same God we are following.

Cinderella's Sister?

Do you sometimes feel like one of Cinderella's stepsisters after the ball? What if the shoe does *not* fit? What if you find yourself identifying with that "workhorse" image, but you suspect the work with which you're horsing around doesn't match your gifts? You may be wondering if your prince will ever come.

Because women can be such workhorses, they often end up in roles that don't fit their gifts. This has always been and will always be true, but it doesn't need to be a source of grave distress. Here's why:

1. Scripture commands all of us to do certain things, whether or not we have a particular spiritual gift. We all are *commanded*—pretty strong word—to have discernment, whether or not we have the gift of discernment of spirits (see 1 Jn 4:1). Apparently also imperative are giving (see Lk 6:38), serving (see Lk 22:26-27; Gal 5:13), being "wise as serpents" (Mt 10:16, RSV), and showing mercy (see Lk 6:36). Paul urges everyone to seek the gift of prophecy (see 1 Cor 14:1). If we read Hebrews 13:2 and Matthew 25:35, we see that hospitality is not reserved only for those with a strong spiritual gift. In the Great Commission (Mt 28:18-20) Jesus says, "Go and make disciples," regardless of giftedness.

Many Scripture passages imply that we should intercede for others, taking our example from Jesus himself. We are also commanded to exhort one another: "Let us encourage one another" (Heb 10:25b; see also Col 3:16). We are supposed to teach in some way, whether or not we are gifted. Fathers are supposed to teach their children (see Eph 6:4); older women are supposed to teach younger women (see Ti 2:4).

Lest this list become a little overwhelming, I hasten to add this point:

2. We can lean on each other. Don't forget that we are members of a body. We are supposed to supplement each other's gifts. If the pastor needs to orchestrate the visit of a traveling choir, he can expect that women will open their homes and someone may volunteer to handle the details. He himself doesn't have to possess either the gifts of hospitality or administration. If a nonteacher has been asked to be the substitute teacher for a classful of eight-year-old boys, she can rely—heavily!—on the instructional materials that have been provided by someone with the gift of teaching.

3. God will equip you with what you need to do a particular job, even if you don't have a matching spiritual gift. Let's say you are asked to lead a women's support group, even though you have always felt more like a follower than a leader. Give it a try. You can be a faithful group leader by using your gifts of encouragement, shepherding, teaching, or service. You will find that you have an adequate measure of leadership, too. When God moves you into unfamiliar territory, he will give you special-grace "anointing" for the new tasks.

Whether or not this is your primary calling, take encouragement from Philippians 2:4-7: "Each of you should look not only to your own interests, but also to the interests of others. Your attitude should be the same as that of Christ Jesus: Who ... made himself nothing, taking the very nature of a servant." Church life must go on. Particularly in small churches, "it is naive to claim everyone should be doing only those things that engage them exclusively in the use of their talents or gifts.... It would be dangerous to limit the work of God's Spirit to one avenue of 'call' or one understanding of how the gifts are evoked."[9]

Heartfelt Encouragement

Especially because we may be serving in less-noticed roles, Christian women need to be alert to opportunities to encourage each other. We read about babies abandoned in poorly run orphanages who are fed and changed like clockwork, but who become listless and eventually die for lack of tender touch and loving words. The same "failure to thrive" can happen to any of us without encouragement.

The church is a living entity made up of individual people. All of us need nurture, encouragement, affirmation, acceptance, and loving direction (see 1 Thes 2:10-12), or we will wither. This is not a foreign concept to women, the life bearers of the church. Specifically, we need to encourage each other in the use of our gifts.

Cart before the horse. Jenny Mellon is a busy, home-schooling mother of five. One day, she was praying for the women of her church, and she pictured a cart in front of a horse. The cart was labelled "gifts" and the horse was labelled "encouragement." The meaning seemed clear: the cart was before the horse in her church, and God wanted her to do something about it.

After prayer and consultation, she decided to initiate a monthly women's breakfast. Her goal was basic: encouragement. She herself wanted to encourage the women by giving little teachings. She also wanted to provide a place for women to become better acquainted so that they could encourage each other. She wanted to hitch that cart (gifts) back behind the horse (encouragement). She drew a horse and a cart on poster paper. At the first breakfast, she had two volunteers hold them and act out her teaching by trading places to put encouragement first.

Encouragement is like food and drink to our spirits. We matter to someone! A listening ear, a shoulder to cry on, advice for attaining and maintaining God's perspective—all help us rise above the personal problems that can derail our fine intentions to use our gifts for others.

Jump starts. Some large churches augment spiritual-gifts training with valuable mentoring programs. Some have established older-to-younger women's mentoring programs that are equally valuable. The tone is pragmatic and upbeat.

However, one ingredient often missing in these programs is an abundance of built-in personal fellowship. Many times, the leaders of such programs are high-energy motivators. They love to train mentors and to spread the benefits of what they've learned. Often these aren't the same people who can tenderly nurture the individuals involved.

New Christians, especially, are infants in their use of gifts. They need "babying." They need to be blessed, Old Testament-style, by their spiritual elders. They need safe, encouraging opportunities to take their first few steps as contributing members of the church. They need people who will draw the gifts out of them, helping them learn to use them and affirming their worth.

Women, sensitive to nuances and nurturers by nature, are absolutely vital to the health of the body of Christ. One-on-one mentoring can take place in a very informal way. Many churches lack the human resources for extensive mentoring programs anyway. Even in those churches with flourishing gift-discovery and implementation programs, informal and personal encouragement cannot be replaced.

To bring the point home: take your spiritual gifts in one hand and your talents and womanly gifts in the other, and use them all to the fullest for the benefit of the people around you!

Six

Into the Blender

If you take nothing else away from this book, please take away this statement: "Your personal gift blend is as unique as your thumbprint." Too many of us expect to be cookie-cutter Christians.

Genevieve states flatly, "I took a test. My gifts are service and giving." Full stop. Period.

Waving my arms wildly, I erupt, "No, wait! There's more! It's bigger and better than you think!"

Service and giving—or whatever gifts you discover—are beautifully blended with your other spiritual gifts, your God-given personality and talents, your cumulative experiences, the fruit of the Spirit in your life, and the liberties or limitations of your current circumstances.

I think of Geri, a young mother who discovered her gift of healing by praying for her feverish baby in the middle of the night. She will never be like healing evangelist Kathryn Kuhlman, praying for hundreds of desperate people each week. Her gift seems to be reserved for close family and friends, and it incorporates her nurses' training and quiet personality.

"[Geri is] God's workmanship, created in Christ Jesus to do good works, which God prepared in advance for [her] to do" (Eph 2:10). Her baby's fever abated and since then, others have been healed through her quiet, personal prayers.

Fifty-seven Varieties (or More!)

Gifts have fuzzy outlines. Sometimes it's impossible to say where one gift leaves off and another picks up. Consider, for example, knowledge and wisdom. "Knowledge is the raw material, but we must have wisdom to know how to use it."[1] Look at faith and intercession—it's sort of a chicken-and-egg question as to which precedes the other.

As they overlap, gifts influence each other. A woman who has the gift of giving and who normally gives most of her money to missions may be expressing a double gifting of giving and missionary ability. Similarly, financial support for educational ministries or seminaries may be the result of a blend of giving and teaching. Giving and exhortation together may impel a woman to support life-changing counseling programs. A "prophetic giver" may target truth-promoting ministries, and an evangelistic giver may prefer to underwrite evangelistic outreaches. The gift of giving combined with administration may result in donations toward ministry facilities, computer equipment, and so on.[2]

The combinations are too numerous to name because they involve not merely gifts two-by-two but many gifts and other factors. "The gifts of the Spirit, though we may consider them apart, are really one graded and indivisible expression of the fullness of God's infinite ability."[3]

Come on in, the water's fine. Just as your personal gifts are intimately blended, your particular gift blend is combined with others' gifts for the task at hand. Our lacks will be supplied by the gifts of others.

In the New Testament, we read about the powerful evangelist Philip. He was evidently lacking somewhat in discernment, to judge by the fact that he probably baptized Simon the magician (see Acts 8:13) before he discerned the state of the man's heart. Philip performed miracles, healings, and exorcisms (read the whole chapter), but he left the job of pastoring the budding churches to others. That was fine. Along came Peter (v. 14) to compensate for Philip's deficiency.

People's gifts build into each other. An evangelist can bring people to faith, but only if there are apostles to establish local churches and pastors and teachers to establish Christians in their faith. "If the prophet ... may be compared to the traveler who discovers new countries, the teacher is like the geographer who combines the scattered results of these discoveries and gives a methodological statement of them."[4] To do God's work, we need each other's gifts.

What a relief not to have to perform equally well in all of them!

"Brand name" or generic? Through spiritual gifts, we are God's hands, feet, and voice. Although it helps us to know what names apply to our gifts, "What difference does it really make if I think a gift is the gift of prophecy and someone else thinks it is the word of knowledge? God is overseeing the whole issue, and He is probably more broadminded and more flexible than for what we give Him credit."[5] The important thing is the continuation of God's work.

Consider deliverance from evil spirits. You might say definitively, "There is a spiritual gift of deliverance and here are the Scriptures to prove it." However, your sister who comes from a church tradition in which exorcism is downplayed can take those same Scriptures and limit her discussion to the gifts of healing or miracles. (After all, to be delivered from an evil spirit *is* a type of healing miracle.) Or perhaps she would fit it under the headings of shepherding/pastoring or evangelism, since deliverance can contribute toward discipleship and evangelism. In any case, no one quibbles about the helpfulness of the gift of discernment of spirits to the operation of the whatever-you-call-it gift.

What matters is that you use your gifts wisely, not so much what names you give them.

Smooth or not so smooth. Take your kitchen blender and pour in cold milk and fresh strawberries. Push "on"—you get strawberry milk. No longer can you separate the two. It's the same with you and your gifts.

Besides your other gifts, talents, and your background, your gifts have been blended with the fruit of the Holy Spirit in your life: "love, joy, peace, patience, kindness, goodness, faithfulness, gentleness and self-control (Gal 5:22b-23), but primarily love, "the greatest of these" (1 Cor 13:13). It doesn't take a theologian to explain the simple logic that the more of God's character you portray, the more your God-given gifts will be used according to your Manufacturer's instructions.

Most of the time, your gift blend seems altogether comfortable to you. However some blends are a little trickier to manage than others.

In my role as a lay pastor to women in my church, I used to suffer from occasional inner turmoil. I prayed for wisdom to understand it. Apparently, my gift blend of exhortation, prophet, and shepherding/pastoring was causing me the trouble. Prophets and exhorters can be blunt, but shepherds (pastors) tend not to want to offend others. As I talked to women, I often took shortcuts to the truth, sometimes bluntly. Even if they received my advice without any objection, I was concerned about being judgmental. The shepherd inside me was standing up to the exhorter. They could have been working together more smoothly if I had better understood the dynamics of their relationship.

No Noisy Gongs

Maturity should be our goal. Spiritual and emotional maturity are inseparably linked with the fruit of the Spirit. We want to be using our gifts with God-given love. None of us wants to be "a noisy gong or a clanging cymbal" (1 Cor 13:1b, RSV), whanging away like a baby with a pot and spoon.

The qualities of love, joy, peace, patience, kindness, goodness, gentleness, faithfulness, and self-control are not bestowed on us full-grown. They are planted in us by the Holy Spirit, and they grow as we yield more and more to the ways of God. They reflect a deep, satisfying relationship with the Spirit of God the Father and Jesus his Son. "Fruitage in the Spirit requires rootage in the Spirit."[6]

No guarantees. People sometimes assume that a powerful spiritual gift guarantees the spiritual maturity of the one who exercises it. Of course this isn't the case. Gifted preachers are brought low in public often enough to prove this point. We can abuse the power of any spiritual gift. It is delegated power, over which we have a sort of "power of attorney."[7]

The early church is full of examples of gifted individuals who hadn't yet reached fruitful maturity. Euodia and Syntyche, the two Philippian women Paul corrects for quarreling, had previously aided the saints in many ways. James and John, if they had not been deterred by Jesus, would have called down fire from heaven to destroy the uncooperative Samaritans. The Corinthian Christians persisted in living up to (or *down* to) the infamous reputation of their city as a hotbed of sin. They "came behind in no gift, but they lagged far behind in the fruit of the Spirit. The presence of such fruit in the life is a far more reliable evidence of spirituality than is the possession and exercise of spectacular spiritual gifts."[8]

In the appendix (Spiritual Gifts Survey for Women), you will note that the characteristics are divided into positive ones and negative ones. Many of the negative points delineate difficulties that an immature believer can encounter in the use of a particular gift. As we grow in the fruit of the Spirit, we can "learn our way out of" such difficulties.

Bread crusts for lunch? First Corinthians 13, the "love chapter," is like the sandwich filling between chapters 12 and 14, both of which discuss spiritual gifts. Employing spiritual gifts without love is like finding two dry pieces of plain bread in your lunchbag instead of a nourishing sandwich. "Make love your aim," writes Paul in 1 Corinthians 14:1 (RSV), "and earnestly desire the spiritual gifts...."

Jesus' beloved John stated succinctly, "Whoever does not love does not know God, because God is love" (1 Jn 4:8). Love, mingled with the godly character traits listed in Galatians 5:22-23, needs to fill all of our gifts.

Test your own use of spiritual gifts by looking for love. When you use your gifts, do people encounter the risen Jesus in you in some small way? Who is being given the attention, you or Jesus? In the last day, Jesus will judge us not by our spectacular gifts, but by whether or not we used them in love (see Mt 7:21-23). If God convicts you of being unloving, don't despair. Whisper your need to your Father, who will forgive you and bring you to new spiritual maturity.

All You Need Is Love?

Suppose you are driving down a deserted piece of road in northern Michigan, and, as my sister Beth did one summer, you come upon an accident. A woman's car has just hit a white-tailed deer. The animal is lying dead in the road, and the weeping woman is standing beside her wrecked car. Would you stop your car, jump out, dash over to the stranger, throw your arms around her lovingly, and gush, "Oh, you need a good hug!"

I hope not! You would do as Beth did—talk reassuringly to the woman, help her assess the situation, and drive her back to her family. That's love in action.

Actions (gifts) aren't worth much without the love, *but* the love can't be expressed without actions.

Humility. The emptier we are of self-effort, the more God's action-motivating love can fill us.

I love the word *humility.* It does not connote humiliation, but rather simple emptiness waiting to be filled and equipped for servanthood. "The power of perfect love forgets itself and finds its blessedness in blessing others—in bearing with and honoring them, however feeble they may be."[9]

Spiritual gifts, by their very nature, are a "manifestation of the Spirit ... for the common good" (1 Cor 12:7). Also, by nature collaborative, they work best when each gifted member of the body contributes his or her bit, in humility. Apollos was an erudite teacher, but he was willing to submit to further instruction by a woman, Priscilla, and her husband, Aquila, who were tentmakers (see Acts 18:24-26). All of them embraced humility in their giving and receiving.

Paradoxically, our spiritual gifts, which can make us fall into pridefulness, can just as easily become a reason for increased humility. We know our loving Father has *bestowed* gifts upon us; we have not earned a single one of them.

Women mentoring women. Younger women or those who are newer believers often want to model themselves after the example of more mature Christian women. Scripture encourages this approach (see Ti 2:3-5). Often, only another woman can help us grow in certain aspects of our lives. It is especially worth noting that similarly gifted women are attracted to each other to give and receive mentoring.

Mentors are in short supply, however. As we move into the second part of this book, you can benefit from the stories of a variety of women. Let them mentor you, encourage you, broaden your thinking, and show you the way to more complete fulfillment in your exercise of your spiritual gifts.

Part II

Gifts in Action

Two of my daughters and I were watching the Miss America competition on TV. Partway through the program, I suppose to build dramatic tension, some clever photographer had created a living collage, a running composite face of the future Miss America. "Which one will it be, ladies and gentlemen?"

Each of the competitors' faces sort of "morphed" into the next. Brunettes with long hair mushroomed into poufy-coiffed blondes as toothy smiles faded into lipsticked pouts, firm chins gave way to delicate ones, blue and brown eyes rotated, and eyebrows went up and down.... It was downright weird. My daughters' reaction: "EEEwww!"

Taken one at a time, each individual face was attractive and glamorous. Run together like that, every one was bordering on grotesque, a good idea that *didn't* work.

I'm taking a similar risk in Part II of this book. In an effort to make two points strongly—namely, that our individual gifts flow together and that each person's gifts are blended within the body of Christ—this section portrays one spiritual gift after another.

You'll find personal stories, "word photographs," if you will. I have inserted limited commentary to link the personal accounts, and I have made every effort to pause the "camera" long enough on each one so you won't have the same stomach-churning reaction that we did when we watched Miss America. As you read along, your appreciation for God's endless creativity will grow.

Note the "Women Only" policy. I have chosen illustrations of *women* using their spiritual gifts, not men, for the reasons I mentioned in Part I. You may well glimpse yourself in one of the vignettes—or you may not. If you don't, that just serves to prove my point further: you are like no one else on earth, past or present. You are a custom-designed creation, unique as your fingerprint.

Let's look at the gifts—in action!

Seven

Gifts in a Prison Camp

Boiled lizard tastes *great!* Try some!" Miriam Skinner exclaimed, proffering a half coconut shell full of gray broth to Sister Mary Evelyn. "I think it tastes like chicken!"

The women, one an American Protestant missionary schoolteacher and the other a Catholic Filipino nun, were soon surrounded by half a dozen ragged companions, all nuns, in the muddy enclosure. The squalor of their surroundings was forgotten as they shared the precious stew.

The condition of their garments betrayed the conditions of their captivity. With only the clothes on their backs, Miriam and most of the sisters had been arrested and taken into captivity thirteen months before. Miriam's tan skirt and white blouse were clinging to her body with sweat, streaked with accumulated soil. Her friends' formerly crisp white habits were dirt-colored, frayed, and hopelessly wrinkled. They were saving their shoes as much as possible, going barefoot except when they were being marched to an interrogation session. Grubby rags were tied around feet and legs to cover tropical sores. Their hair, matted and full of lice, had been chopped off as short as possible with the *bolo* (jungle knife) they kept hidden in the stinking latrine, the same knife Miriam had just used to disembowel the unfortunate lizard.

The eight women felt vulnerable all the time. Their rickety hut was constructed of split bamboo and roofed with a leaky combination of old thatch and pieces of packing crates. Their only bedding was the clothing they wore. When dysentery struck, they prayed and waited it out; there was no medicine available and no defense against the giant blue-bottle flies that carried the disease. Sister Rose coughed all the time with chronic bronchitis. Vitamin deficiencies were beginning to take a serious toll.

Now it was July, 1944, the beginning of the rainy season. The heavy rains were starting to flood the latrine again. Miriam tried to look on the bright side: "At least the stench keeps Stoneface and Brickfist farther away!"

That morning, Sister Li Wen, who was half Chinese, had caught a glimpse of a headline in the Japanese-language newspaper that had been rolled up under a guard's arm. "I think it said, *PRIESTS, MISSIONARIES ARRESTED IN MANILA,*" she reported. "It was another big sweep."

Between once-daily interrogations and twice-daily meals, their two Japanese guards (nicknamed "Stoneface" and "Brickfist" by their captives) let them fend for themselves. Lately, they had even let the women move one of their two oil-drum cookstoves into the enclosure, furnishing each captive with a daily shovelful of charcoal and a bucketful of water. Why should *they* do women's work? They were disgruntled with this assignment—trained soldiers of the Japanese imperial army, relegated to guard duty for a gaggle of filthy females! Their instructions had been, "Keep them alive and keep them afraid."

Two times a day for thirteen months, "Stoneface" grudgingly ladled out thin vegetable broth into the women's battered bowls. The broth and less than a cup of cooked rice per prisoner were the allotment for each meal. Sometimes the broth was a little greasier and there were strings of unidentifiable meat in it, probably *carabao* (a kind of water buffalo). The women had learned to augment their meager diet with whatever came to hand: edible weeds, insects, or any hapless small creature.

Miriam's family back in the States had no idea what had become of her. All they knew was that her letters home had become much less frequent and then had ceased abruptly after Manila had fallen to the Japanese in January 1942. They prayed for her day and night, hoping against hope that she was still alive.

Miriam had gone to the Philippines in 1937 as a teacher in one of the mission schools, fulfilling a lifelong dream to serve God overseas doing what she loved best—teaching children. Her newsy letters, sent weekly to her parents and younger siblings in Depression-weary South Dakota, had painted vivid word-pictures of a tropical paradise.

Her mother used to share the letters with her circle of friends, women at her country church. "I've always said Miriam was meant to be a missionary teacher! She doesn't mind discomforts or strange foods as long as she can be surrounded by children. She says she doesn't even want to be married because she's married to Jesus—and to the work he's called her to do."

Miriam was a bit of an "ugly duckling"—square of body, pug-nosed, brusque in mannerisms. Children, however, didn't find her unattractive; they could sense her love. In the mission school, when Miriam crossed the sunny courtyard, they flocked to her like chicks to a mother hen.

In Manila, rumblings of war had become so commonplace—while school life went along so pleasantly—that it had been hard to take the rumors seriously. Before the surprise Japanese attack on Pearl Harbor on December 7, 1941, everyone had thought that the more strategic Manila Harbor, protected as it was by the Bataan peninsula, would have been the most likely site for an initial strike. For that reason, Miriam's family and her denominational mission board had urged her to consider a stateside assignment. Miriam had weighed the decision. Many of the other teachers did leave before the school year started in 1941, especially those who were married with children of their own.

But Miriam, enchanted by the islands and the resilient people with their Malay, Chinese, Spanish, and Indian heritage, had decided to stay on. After all, someone had to take up the extra teaching duties. The nearby Roman Catholic boarding school was short-staffed too, so the teachers from both schools started to teach some combined classes. She and Sister Mary Evelyn, a native Filipino, as were most of the school's Catholic nuns, had become acquainted when Miriam volunteered to take over the English class in the other school.

One bright December day, the school administrator had burst into the teachers' common room waving the daily newspaper: *ONE HUNDRED JAPANESE WARSHIPS HEADING FOR PHILIPPINE WATERS, ROME REPORTS.*

One thing had led swiftly to another. First, the devastating but somehow unreal news about Pearl Harbor. Miriam, so far from home, heard that her country had declared war on Japan. The Japanese had had the advantage from the beginning. San Pablo, only forty-five miles away, fell to the Japanese on December 30. Manila was not a safe place to be.

Before conquering General Masaharu Homma marched into Manila on January 2, all the boarding students had been sent home to the relative safety of their own families. Most of Miriam's American and British civilian friends had been detained at Santo Tomas University internment camp. Filipino refugees had poured in from the countryside. In exchange for their own relative freedom, the missionaries and teachers at both schools had been required to house them in their dormitories.

So far, so good. Every day was filled with hard work and a hundred details. Besides caring for the refugee families, Miriam and the sisters made it their responsibility to collect foodstuffs and supplies for the internees at Santo Tomas and eventually for the American and Allied POWs at nearby Bilibid Prison, a seventy-seven-year-old Spanish-built fortress. With a combination of good timing and, Miriam suspected, angelic assistance, they could get a few baskets of vegetables and medicines into even that forbidding place.

Many of the Filipino refugees housed at the school were fellow Christians. Most had friends and relatives in other refugee housing managed by priests and pastors. A cooperative network was growing. Soon, an underground resistance movement began to gain momentum throughout the capital city.

Miriam helped them sometimes. Her compact frame and nondescript dark hair aiding the disguises, she had posed first as a doctor and then as a simple-minded maid, passing messages for her friends in the resistance.

She found out too late that she wasn't very well suited to subterfuge. Yes, she was fearless and focused, but she was a bit too trusting, especially of her neighbors. On June 5, 1943, an assassination attempt was made on Dr. José P. Laurel, who later became occupation president of the Philippines. As a result the Japanese army tightened security, and civilians were stopped for questioning. Miriam had been arrested right on Quezon Avenue after a local "friend" betrayed her for sixteen Filipino pesos (about eight U.S. dollars).

With only the clothes she was wearing and a handkerchief in her pocket, she had been trucked with a group of anxious prisoners to the garage of a bus depot for one sleepless night, then to this small outpost on the edge of the jungle, which had become her new home. Sister Mary Evelyn and three of the other nuns were arrested and confined on the next day. Now there were eight of them here, kept isolated from other prisoners of war for unknown reasons. They had been told that they were charged with "harboring resistance workers."

As they savored their lizard stew, the women showed the effects of their ongoing interrogation. Sister Letecia was missing two front teeth. Delicate Sister Conception was still chewing slowly because of a poorly mended broken jaw. Once-rotund Sister Ruth was bent over and stiffened with relentless back pain, her habit hanging down from her shoulders like dirty surgical drapery. Miriam couldn't see her own black and blue cheeks and forehead, the yellow and brown of old bruises beneath the new ones—she could only try to rinse away the aching with a little precious water.

Their Japanese captors slapped them so much, so hard! There were no more answers for the daily interrogations; the women had told them everything already. Even the Japanese interpreter had tried to stop the abuse. Yet the soldiers kept hammering away at them, trying to worm out more information, desperate to please their superiors by presenting at least the appearance of successful interrogation. At least, with the exception of a few cigarette burns to their arms, the beatings hadn't given way to worse punishments.

"Quick! Hide it! He's coming!"

A white cloud of cigarette smoke was hanging in the humid air above the tall gate as one of the guards rattled the fastening.

The one they called "Brickfist" came in dragging a burlap sack.

"Ymphth!" he grunted through his teeth as he tossed the sack into a mud puddle, then turned on his heel and left.

The women approached the sack eagerly. Even the burlap itself was a welcome gift. Inside: Two Red Cross parcels, broken open and raided, the first they had seen! Cocoa powder! Dry milk! A tin of sardines! And, wonder of wonders, a spool of white thread and a single sewing needle! Never mind that it was already corroded with the humidity, now they could mend what was left of their ragged clothing. Scattered in the bottom of the sack, the women's astonished eyes beheld another wonder: a dozen *tampons!*

"Of all things!" laughed Miriam. "Something those guys weren't interested in. We hardly ever need them either...." But of course they kept them.

Now she and the nuns could repair their tattered clothing. The needle became a symbol of their determination to live and not yield easily to intimidation or the fear of death. Whatever happened in the long run, they were not going to give in to hopelessness.

To avoid having their precious needle confiscated, the women took turns mending their own garments when they went to the latrine, the one place in which the guards never set foot. A stitch here, a stitch there, the rotten fabric gradually began to hold together better. Between visits to the outhouse, they kept the needle stuck right up into one of the Red Cross tampons, which they stored above the doorway. (One rainy day, Sister Letecia had noted that just there, the unpainted wood doorframe met an upright piece in the shape of a cross.) Of all places, the reeking latrine had become a refuge and a place of hope.

One midafternoon, Stoneface and Brickfist entered the bare yard together, carrying between them the usual steaming and sloshing soup kettle. "But," the women murmured, "this isn't mealtime...."

"Speh-shahl!" Stoneface leered in broken English. "Eat!"

The stack of bowls was brought out from inside the hut. The soup was ladled into them.

"EAT!" bellowed Brickfist, raising his powerful arms.

The women, always weak with hunger, complied meekly, tipping their bowls to their mouths. The soup tasted better than usual. They drank it gratefully. What was in it this time? Thin strips of some special vegetable?

"Stop!" gagged Sister Martha. "They've put *bamboo* in it!"

It was true. Each woman spat out her last mouthful of soup—and tasted her own blood. The guards laughed maliciously and slapped each other on the back. What a fine joke!

"Shredded bamboo can kill you! It cuts you up inside!" the Filipino nuns told Miriam, spitting blood. "Maybe this amount wasn't enough to kill us, but, but...."

I shall not die, but live, and declare the works of the Lord. The words from Psalm 118 leapt to Miriam's mind. Up until now she had tried not to think about death, especially her own. In this hellish place, *hope* was their anchor. Giving up hope amounted to suicide—hopelessness was the most deadly disease of all. Without their strong faith in a loving, ever-present God, none of the women could have survived even this long. Now, with the taste of her own blood in her mouth, Miriam realized with a rush that *death did not make her afraid.* She felt liberated from all fear. All she cared about was pleasing the One who had saved her from the second death.

"OK, maybe you've killed us all," she said quietly to the mocking guards. "We forgive you."

The men had no idea what the English words meant. They chortled.

The other seven women, in shock, daubed their reddening lips with their fingers. At Miriam's words, two of them fell to their knees and crossed themselves, leaving bloodstains on their shoulders and foreheads.

That night was a long one. The soup bowls were filled many times with bloody vomit. Before sunrise, little Sister Li Wen whispered weakly, "There is a Chinese proverb: 'To accept death with courage at an impassioned moment is easy; to choose death after long deliberation is difficult.' I accept death because my Lord did." And she expired on the bloodstained floor. At dawn, the guards took her body away, unceremoniously, in a wheelbarrow.

Somehow, the remaining women gathered their strength day by day. No one else died, although they all had private thoughts that death (and certainly heaven) would be much preferred to the debilitating internal and external injuries the guards had inflicted on them.

One sweltering day in August, Miriam was in the latrine, trying to mend her threadbare underpants. There wasn't much left to sew together, unfortunately. Suddenly she heard the sound of a truck just outside the gate. The brakes squealed and men's voices spoke rapidly.

Her mind registered everything at once: *We're being moved!* Peering out a crack in the wall, she saw Japanese soldiers burst through the gate and stride briskly toward the bamboo hut, collaring Sister Ruth as they went. Sounds of scrambling came from inside the ramshackle building, which rocked and swayed as the soldiers tore off the door. *No time to collect anything! Help me, Jesus!*

A wild idea presented itself. Thrusting the precious needle and its bit of thread back into the center of the tubular tampon, she inserted it right into her body, deftly and carefully. Pulling her fragile underwear back on, she opened the door and stepped into the grip of one of the soldiers.

The women had no way of knowing it then, but their transfer marked the beginning of the end of their captivity. Trucked to Bilibid Prison for a mass trial on August 15, 1944, for the first time in more than a year they saw some of their old friends. Ninety of the resistance sympathizers, many of them missionaries and religious workers, were subjected to a general trial. Thirty of them, including several middle-aged American women missionaries and one Filipino nun from the Immaculate Conception Convent in Manila, received the death sentence. They were beheaded two weeks later in the Chinese cemetery of Manila.

Most of the others were returned with haste to their former quarters in various prisoner of war camps—except the ailing Miriam and her friends, who were housed in the POW hospital cellblock at Bilibid for the duration of the war. (Yes, the precious sewing needle continued to be a useful bit of equipment, shared widely.)

Manila was liberated after five more months of war. Miriam, after tearful good-byes to her friends, none of whom she ever saw again, was moved by hospital ship to San Francisco. Eventually, she returned to her anxious family in South Dakota. She recovered slowly.

After two years, she returned to teaching and eventually found a good position as a Spanish teacher in a Christian boarding school in Washington, D.C.

From time to time, she shared parts of her story with her

fascinated pupils. She suffered lifelong intestinal problems because of the shredded bamboo. Her memories and her pain were her only "souvenirs"; the precious needle had been shared with others in Bilibid to such an extent that it had been lost. As she told her story to new generations of students, she often offered to mend their school clothes at the same time.

"This is not a difficult chore; a sewing needle is always going to be special to me," she would say, making quick stitches.

"If I had died in the war, some people might have called me a 'martyr.' Martyrs are people who are killed because they are Christians. I didn't die, did I? Some people call me a *living* martyr. I don't know about that. I think I'm just a lady—sometimes crabby because of my tummyaches—who loves Jesus and who loves teaching all of *you*.

"I do know one thing: it isn't so special just to escape getting killed. Survival isn't worth much if you're still afraid of death." Having earned their rapt attention, she would tell again the old, old story about the One who won victory over both fear and death.

Martyrdom Is Not Dead

Though Miriam is not her real name, she is a real person. Death came to her when she was about sixty-five, just after she retired from her teaching job in Washington. One of her former pupils told me her story, and I felt it deserved special attention in a book about women and their spiritual gifts.[1] Better than dry text could do, her experiences illustrate that spiritual gifts, especially martyrdom, are not dead.

Some jokingly state that martyrdom is the spiritual gift you use only once.[2] No one knows what percentage of Christians have been given the spiritual gift of martyr; perhaps it only becomes evident in soon-to-be-martyred ones. We read that between 160,000 and 300,000 Christian men and women *every year* around the world give their lives for their faith.[3] Surely it stands to reason that our God, who supplies our every need, would supply a supernatural gift of courage to undergo suffering and death when we are required to face such ultimate trials.

Why do I use Miriam's story to illustrate the gift of martyrdom? After all, her life went on for years after she was released from prison. Is it in fact possible to be some kind of "living martyr"?

Some people think so. Sister Li Wen did die. So did those thirty Christians who were beheaded. Miriam, however, lived on. If her health had permitted, her heart's desire would have been to return to Manila. As it was, she suffered an ongoing, painful martyrdom. Her slow death from her prison injuries was made more difficult because she was banished from her beloved Filipino children. The only thing Washington, D.C., had in common with Manila was the August humidity.

She retained her missionary zeal, living out the Greek meaning of the word *martyr*, which is "witness." She kept loving, kept forgiving, kept serving with her other gifts—notably teaching, celibacy, and likely evangelism—until the year of her death. I imagine that when she arrived at the throne, she received the commendation we all hope to hear, "'Well done, good and faithful servant'" (Mt 25:21).

Whether or not it makes it onto most of the lists of spiritual gifts, martyrdom is the all-or-nothing gift.

However, many of us disqualify ourselves from using even the most commonplace gifts. Don't skip the next chapters, even if you think you are about as gifted as an evangelist as you are as a martyr. You might be surprised!

Eight

Gifts From Country Club to Shantytown

In 1956, Wilma Stanchfield was a vivacious young woman living in Minneapolis with her well-to-do husband, Roald, and his three children by another marriage. Their life was satisfying. None of them were Christians. Then in a freak camping accident, both she and her husband were struck by lightning while watching a thunderstorm from their tent. Wilma has told the story in her book, *Struck by Lightning, Then by Love.*[1]

By all odds, they both should have died, but instead they had life-changing near-death experiences, recovered, and began a search for God. "However," Wilma emphasizes, "knowing there is a God and actually knowing God are two entirely different things."

They tried to repay this God who had saved their lives by volunteering for an increasing number of "good works." They joined a church, Wilma says, because she "liked the pastor's accent" and because he would let them believe anything they wanted. They worked tirelessly for good causes. But for ten long years, Wilma and Roald were, in spiritual terms, "dull of hearing" (Heb 5:11, KJV).

After that decade of trying to work off their debt to God, they were approached by new neighbors who were Christians.

This couple saw significance in their near-death experience. But no way were Wilma and Roald going to let themselves "get saved"—they felt they were Christians already, thank you very much. Then Joanie, the wife, invited Wilma to a luncheon at a country club, sponsored by a group called Christian Women's Clubs.

Wilma writes, "When I walked into that club with my neighbor, I had it all figured out. I was supposedly already a Christian, you understand—I was known for doing all these good things, and I belonged to a big church and the best clubs. I had been baptized, catechized, confirmed, and the whole bit. So I walked in with my guard up. I was all set to deal with the 'pickle noses' and the 'little buns of hair' and their uptight propositions."

Instead, an attractive speaker explained how she herself had come to know the living Jesus, and how her listeners could do the same. Wilma was "struck by love," and soon she stepped into the fullness of new life. Before long her husband and her stepdaughter followed her.

After two years of avid participation in a new church and a Bible study, Wilma herself was invited to become a speaker with Christian Women's Clubs.

She loved it. An extrovert by nature and good with words, she not only had a strong desire to spread the gospel, but she had a dramatic story to share as well. Many women responded to her message. Speaking-engagement invitations began to come in from other cities.

By the late 1970s, the focus of many of her engagements had shifted, and most were with groups of Christian women, many of whom were involved in the charismatic renewal. Because of its mission (reaching unchurched women with the gospel of Jesus), Christian Women's Clubs had a policy that prohibited its speakers from making public appearances with religiously controversial groups. Even though Wilma sometimes referred to these new speaking venues as "Christian Bless-Me Clubs," she was excited about her new invitations, and she resisted following the policy. "You can't tell me where to speak!" she protested. With more than enough new speaking invitations from Christian conferences, seminars, and broadcasts to keep her busy, she terminated her work as an evangelistic speaker with Christian Women's Clubs.

Wilma expected to thrive in her broadening world. Instead, she became increasingly miserable. She still enjoyed speaking, especially the Bible-teaching aspects, but something had died inside her heart. Sometimes she was asked to lay hands on women and to pray over them after her presentations. She was gracious about doing so, but quite uncomfortable. She knew she was not gifted to do that. For seven years, she was restless and unhappy.

Finally one day she realized that she had not led a single woman to Christ in all that time. The work that previously had been her "food and drink" was on the shelf. There was no one to evangelize at a Christian conference! Suddenly, she realized that the relative spiritual fruitlessness of the previous seven years could be traced directly to her self-willed rebellion against her true calling.

"I ate humble pie, and asked to be reinstated as a speaker with Christian Women's Clubs," reports Wilma. "They took me back, and at my very first luncheon engagement, unchurched women were converted.

"Now I don't travel as much as I used to, but I still speak about fifty times a year—to groups of non-Christian women in secular settings, often country clubs. I want to remember my lesson. I consider that seven years to be part of the necessary growing process. I have nothing against all-Christian groups, and I still speak to such gatherings sometimes. However, evidently my gift of evangelism has to have an outlet. Wherever I go, women come to the Lord! All this and heaven too!"

Wilma is an evangelist with a capital *E.* Her energetic personality and life circumstances make her extra persuasive and winsome to women, especially those who are leery of entering a "religious" atmosphere. She is also gifted with teaching (she has taught Bible studies since 1967). Her gift of mercy is channeled primarily toward the women she is trying to reach. She notices certain other spiritual gifts (such as giving) in action from time to time, and she would certainly attribute much of her biblical knowledge and life wisdom to God, whether or not they are actual spiritual gifts.

But for the most part, she would say "Not my gift" in response to the following gifts on our list. Miracles—nope. Helps—probably not. Missionary—not unless she could call ministering to the country-club set a "cross-cultural experience." Service—been there, done that, nope. Healing—probably not. Administration—yawn. Exorcism—I don't think so. Voluntary poverty or apostle or celibacy—triple nope!

Wilma's happy about her lacks, because they help her focus on her true calling.

Hand-to-Mouth

Wilma Stanchfield clearly does not lack material provision. Beverley Moore does. She lives in a garbage-dump shanty in Riverton City, Jamaica, with her nine children and her mother. But the gift of faith illuminates Bev's dark face in spite of the difficulties of her daily existence. For her, the only hard life is one that's lived without faith in God.

She greets callers on the crumbling front stoop of her tumbledown shanty and brushes the flies away from her baby's head as she says, "Listen, when you know God, you don't talk about a hard life.... To others it looks hard, but it looks easy to me because I don't watch what is hard.... [I] watch the Creator and what he can do for me."

Bev is 100 percent sure that what God promises, he will do. Bev discusses her daily needs with her Provider moment by moment: "At home, at church, on the bus, when I scrub clothes—anywhere, I pray. Just talk to God silent and he understands everything, every little grunt." His provision has never failed her, although by American middle-class standards, it is insufficient. Bev has never known anything but struggle—with hunger, sickness, a deteriorating shack with no amenities, fatigue—but she replaces complaints with thanksgiving. "I thank God for keeping me, for carrying me, for everything he is doing for me. I thank him for the food he has provided, for the clothes, for these children. Yeah man, I thank him because he's the one who have given me everything, the great and the small!" To her, the greatest provision of all is God's salvation, and she has passed on a saving faith to her children and to many others.[2]

Daily bread. Like Beverley, Reville Johnson trusts God for everything. Unlike Beverley, she lives in relative comfort, although she has known what "hand-to-mouth" means. She is a pastor's wife who has developed an abiding gift of faith.

Today her three children are grown, but when they were small, her husband was in seminary in Georgia. For the first two years of his schooling, Reville supported the family by teaching school, but in the third year, she quit her teaching job to stay home and take care of the children. They had no regular income.

Week after week, Reville had no milk, no groceries, and no money to buy them. She would gather her little ones around her in a circle and lead them in a prayer of faith for what they needed. "Dear Lord, we need you to meet our small but important needs. I believe that you don't want the children to go hungry. I pray that you'll send the money to get the milk and the food we need. Thank you, Lord."

The provision would come, time after time. Reville would open the mail, and there would be a check for $50 or a little cash, and they would have their food and milk for another week.

Reville's gift of faith has never stopped growing. Although she and her husband have rarely been unemployed since then, to this day she prays about everything. If she needs a dress, she spends time with the Lord before going shopping, goes out with a modest sum—and finds what she needs for that exact amount or less. More important, Reville endures in faith when most of us would throw in the towel. When she was battling cancer a few years ago, she continually prayed for others in treatment. She is a "closet warrior"—and that does not mean only that her closet is full of prayed-for dresses!

The gift of faith can be contagious. In other words, being around someone with this gift can make one's own "faith temperature" rise. Without boasting about spiritual victories, these folks radiate a stability that comes from an unquestioning trust in the sovereignty of God. To whom do you instinctively turn in a moment of crisis? Who do you know who unleashes your trust in the Lord? That person almost certainly possesses the gift of faith. She knows that even if the answer to her prayers is "no," God remains the One to trust in all circumstances.

If you yourself don't feel you have a particular gift of faith, I hope you have a friend who does, like Reville or Beverley. Her faith will build yours up. We need each other's gifts.

Down-Home Hospitality

"Good *morning!*" Gloria beamed. "*Do* come in!"

The caller hesitated. Did he have the wrong time of day? Here he was in his pastoral collar, notebook tucked under his arm, ready to discuss the new church directory, and there *she* was, her plumpness enveloped in a chenille bathrobe, yellow rubber gloves dripping soapsuds.

"I said, 'Come *in,*'" she insisted, gesturing with both wet hands. "The kids had a day off school, so we all slept in. The house is a mess, but the coffeepot's on. Here, let me pour you a cup, Pastor, then I'll leave you for just a minute. Meg will walk over now that you're here. She's been on the lookout for your car so we could have our little meeting."

"Thanks, Gloria. Where should I sit?"

"Oh, why don't you just move last night's paper off the recliner; it's the best seat.... Here's Meg already. In here, Meg. Pastor's got a cup of coffee. Help yourself while I quick go and change."

Cut.

Would you feel comfortable if you were Gloria?

If you were a guest, would you feel comfortable in her house? Unless you are a complete neatnik, probably you *would,* despite the disorderly surroundings. Why?

Is it because Gloria makes *your* housekeeping look good? Because you like chenille bathrobes and rubber gloves? Because her welcome is so genuine?

It's her *hospitality,* right? Whatever I think of Gloria's skills as a housewife, I have to appreciate her hospitality. Why, she almost seems blind to things that might embarrass another woman. She focuses on *me,* on my comfort. I like that.

If you think "hospitality," who and what come to mind—Martha Stewart? *House Beautiful?* Does the idea of inviting someone over for dinner give you hives, or does it put sparkle in your eyes?

Gloria (and many, many other women) have the gift of hospitality big-time. It easily overrides other considerations such as a messy house.

She is blooming where she has been planted, never mind the weeds. So can you, whether you were "born with a silver spoon in your mouth" or don't know where your next meal is coming from.

Our God wants us to use the spiritual gifts he has given us wherever we are. Can you be happy about not only your messy house but your other lacks? What if you find it difficult to use your spiritual gifts because you have so many personal problems? Can God use you as well as he uses a Miriam, a Wilma, a Beverley, a Reville, or a Gloria? Read on about Anna, Maribeth, Kimmie, and others.

Nine

Gifts, Against All Odds

"No you don't, young lady!" snarled the big man, through twisted lips.

Smack! His hand slapped her plump little cheek like an explosion, spinning her face to the side so fast that her blonde pigtails stood straight out.

"Just for that, I'm going to keep your bedroom light on all night from now on. You're not sneakin' out of here, no way!"

Fifteen years later, Anna (not her real name) finally made her escape in the time-honored way; she grew up and left home. But "home," especially the abuse of her alcoholic father, never left her sensitive mind and spirit. Anna had an exceptional mind, an intense ability to focus on her studies, and great physical attractiveness. She didn't want marriage, as it so often is, to be her ticket to freedom from her troubled family—she was far too afraid of all men after the sexual and physical abuse her father had visited on her.

Education was her one-way ticket, accompanied by religion. A scholarship to a parochial school had introduced her to Catholicism. Kind and wise confessors and teachers had helped her find a faith to call her own. For a while, she toyed with the idea of the celibate life (how appealing! how safe!), then abandoned it after she became convinced that God wanted her to work through her fears before she decided her future. Several years of self-help and professional counseling, all in a strong Christian context, helped her out of the depths—and fed a new desire to become a Christian counselor herself.

Wisdom seemed to have been poured into her in spite of her decidedly *un*wise parents. Even when Anna was depressed, which did happen more often for her than for other women, she exhibited a maturity beyond her years.

"I can help others better because I have suffered so much," she would say. "God must know what he's doing."

He seemed to give her extra helpings of love. After she had become the youngest master's graduate in the history of her college's psychology department, she was awarded a special grant to study at a university in England. At a department tea, she met Charles, a history professor and lifelong Anglican churchman, who brought her home to meet his wife and two small children. They lavished affection upon her. Their home became a refuge for her in a foreign country. Eventually, Charles and his wife Evie invited her to move out of her one-room flat into their spare bedroom. Anna wished she had been born into that family.

Every day before taking the bus to the university, she walked by herself to a small parish church to attend morning Mass. She remained scrupulous about every detail of religious observance, which included making regular confessions to the parish priest, Father Joseph, who happened also to be a friend of Charles. He was a good one to talk to, which was another evidence of God's love to Anna. Both men respected her integrity and intelligence and took a fatherly interest in her welfare.

One gray afternoon after an appointment with Father Joseph, Anna was putting on her boots and coat. The priest casually mentioned a difficult letter he was trying to write to a Doubting Thomas who was a psychologist. He had spent most of his morning trying to answer this man's hefty challenges and questions.

Anna narrowed her eyes and stopped buttoning her coat. "Why did you spend so much time doing that?" she asked. "Can't you tell that he doesn't really want those kinds of answers? He wants to hear about God's love."

"But he didn't ask anything that would lead me to think so," said the kind priest.

"I just know that's what he needs. I'm usually right about such things," responded the young woman.

This was a new side of Anna! "What *else* do you 'just know'?" he queried.

"Oh, only the things God seems to want to show me. For instance, I know that you are a little too dependent upon what men such as this one think of your education. I think you should stop trying so hard to impress him with your scholarliness."

"I haven't told you anything before today about this man. How can you attribute such motives to me?" Father Joseph was beginning to feel a bit defensive.

"I know you haven't told me. I can just pick these things up. I can tell you're even a little intimidated by my education. You don't need to be. I respect your judgment regardless of how many degrees you have, Father."

Anna left that day feeling a little shaken. This was the first time she had expressed such discernments, even though she recognized the pattern in herself. "It's not just my training," she mused. "I think it might be from God." She decided, when she got home, to borrow the family concordance and look up some Scripture having to do with judgment, discernment, and spiritual gifts.

"Mom always said, 'Judge not lest ye be judged,'" she was

thinking. "I'd better watch out.... Maybe I'm supposed to *pray* more than *say*.... I sure seem to know who's sincere and who isn't.... Sometimes on the bus I can feel evil emanating from certain people, and I don't know how to pray for that.... Help, Lord! I need to understand this better!"

Anna wasn't as familiar with the Bible as she wanted to be. The word *wisdom* in the concordance netted her almost too many references to look up, but she decided to check them all. The word *discernment* was easier to check. After becoming almost lost in the cross-references for wisdom in the book of Proverbs, she came upon 1 Corinthians 12, the "gift chapter." She had just read 1 Corinthians 2:12, "Now we have received not the spirit of the world, but the Spirit which is from God, that we might understand the gifts bestowed on us by God" (RSV). Then chapter 12 yielded the following verses:

> To each is given the manifestation of the Spirit for the common good. To one is given through the Spirit the utterance of wisdom, and to another the utterance of knowledge according to the same Spirit,... to another the ability to distinguish between spirits.... All these are inspired by one and the same Spirit, who apportions to each one individually as he wills.
>
> 1 CORINTHIANS 12:7-8, 10b, 11, RSV

This was helpful! When she had a chance to talk with them, she took her findings to both Father Joseph and Charles. "Could it be some kind of a *gift*? Wow! I thought only real saintly people had gifts from God." The two men didn't know much about spiritual gifts either, but they began to read the Bible with that in mind, because they were concerned for Anna's welfare. They read about Peter, Ananias, and Sapphira in

Acts 5 and about Paul, Silas, and the slave girl in Acts 16. They had known these stories but had never thought about them in terms of their relevance to discernment or to modern-day spiritual gifts.

Charles, who enjoyed reading about religious history, showed Anna something more. In the university library, he had been reading about the early Puritans in England, and now he could put some of what he had read into the new context of "spiritual gifts."

He brought home some excerpts from a book about Margaret Baxter, wife of seventeenth-century Puritan pastor Richard Baxter. When her husband was presented with knotty "cases of conscience," he had discovered that she was gifted to untangle the situations with incisive wisdom:

> She was better at resolving a case of conscience than most divines that ever I knew in all my life. I often put cases to her which she suddenly so resolved as to convince me of some degree of oversight in my own resolution. Abundance of difficulties were brought me, some about restitution, some about injuries, some about references, some about vows, some about marriage promises, and many such like; and she would lay all the circumstances presently together, compare them, and give me a more exact resolution than I could do.[1]

Quite likely, Charles theorized, Margaret Baxter had used more than her feminine intuition to be able to deliver such wisdom so frequently.

In all her reading and thinking, Anna got confused in her effort to define which spiritual gifts she possessed. Wisdom? Discernment? Knowledge? Even prophecy? "Maybe they're all combined somehow," she reasoned finally. "The important thing is that I try not to get off God's track whenever I think I know what he's thinking."

Anna is still growing. She wants her spiritual gifts to help her help others.

We Need More Annas

People have always been deceived by counterfeit spiritualities. We are warned in 2 Corinthians 11:14 that Satan disguises himself as an angel of light, yet regular churchgoers read their horoscopes in the newspaper and let New Age practices filter into their daily life. False prophets capture us with their charm and erudition. We want to know things we don't need to know.

What we need is discernment. Some, Anna among them, are gifted with this ability to distinguish what is from human nature, from God, or even from the devil. Discernment includes not only discernment of evil spirits or angels, but also being able to tell natural "spirits" in people. People with this gift often can name a person's underlying motives, good or bad. They can distinguish goodness from evil, even when both look "right." They can tell the difference between demonic activity and very similar-looking symptoms of mental illness. This is a lot more than natural intuition at work, although I suspect that we women often throw that into the mix as well.

As a woman with the gift of discernment enters a room full of people, she often can sense the prevailing mood of the group, sometimes even tracing the responsibility for the mood to one individual. She may or may not know what to do about it.

Sometimes this gift can seem like a liability. A speaker may stand in the pulpit and deliver a well-reasoned and well-expressed message. Mrs. Discerner misses most of the message because she is uncomfortable with the underlying pride she sees in the speaker. Later, she may say to her husband in exasperation, "Oh, if only he hadn't been so cocksure of himself! A little humility would have gone a long way to enhance that message!" Only to have her husband look at her blankly or even take her to task for what he thinks is judgmentalism.

Mrs. Discerner and Anna need to pray for more wisdom for when to speak and when not to. Whether or not they are equipped with the gift of intercession, they can learn to turn some of those discernments into effective prayers without ever saying a word aloud to anyone. If they have the additional gift of exhortation, they may more often find ways to express encouraging observations to others. God will lean hard on their own motives. He wants the gift to be expressed with his love and mercy.

Women who have these gifts don't have X-ray eyes! They can only know what God's Spirit gives them. Sometimes they make mistakes; there is a lot to learn. Lessons learned from life experiences and education can strengthen these "perceiving" gifts. Discernment can be enhanced by natural common sense and keen powers of observation.

A prophetic gift often goes hand in hand with the gift of discernment, to the degree that the individual can't separate the two. In some churches a "word of knowledge" is essentially a prophetic discernment delivered for all to hear. Such a word from a woman with the gift of exhortation will usually be a loving, if incisive, commendation or reassurance to those for whom it is intended. Such a word from a woman with a gift of intercession may be phrased as a spontaneous prayer.

For many other women, this sort of gift will express itself in quiet, personal words like the ones Anna spoke to Father Joseph. How many wise and discerning women stand behind husbands who are pastors or church leaders, gently prodding them to see God's hand in confusing matters? How many more would do it better if they knew it was a gift from God? Whether or not your upbringing was "dysfunctional," you too could be an Anna.

Handicap Accessible

Maribeth's body is rigid and contorted with cerebral palsy, but her spirit is beautiful. There is nothing at all wrong with her intelligence!

From her earliest memory, she has coped with her disability with a combination of frustration and acceptance. Her faith, nurtured in her by godly parents, sustains her and keeps her from giving in to bitterness or rage at the seeming senselessness of her affliction.

When Maribeth was growing up in St. Louis, she went to school with the "regular kids." She got along surprisingly well, in spite of almost daily patronizing remarks or childish ridicule. Many people couldn't bring themselves to look her in the eye when they encountered her in public. She longed to be *known*, to be appreciated, to make a difference in the world.

Besides her family, which included an older brother and a younger sister, there were always a few friends who could be counted on. They took the time to listen to Maribeth's tortured speech, to understand her. One of them, a high school English teacher named Mrs. Keller, went to extraordinary lengths to help Maribeth develop her innate skill with words. She helped Maribeth obtain a specially equipped computer on which to write her papers. She introduced her to a wide variety of authors and types of writing, challenging her with extra-credit assignments galore.

It always seemed ironic to Mrs. Keller that here was a girl who could barely speak two intelligible words in succession, yet she seemed to be developing into quite a wordsmith. "You can *do* something with this skill, Maribeth," the teacher would insist. "Keep up the good work!"

After high school, the only reasonable option for Maribeth was to remain living at home with her family and to enroll in the local community college—only one course, because she needed to spend so much of every day just getting from place to place and doing ordinary tasks. She enrolled in a journalism class taught by an uncompromising former newspaperman.

"I don't care if you're busy with toddlers at home or a full-time job, to pass my class, you're gonna have to *work!* In addition to class time, I expect everyone to go out and show some *hustle.* You'll get several major assignments during the semester. To get an 'A' in my class, you're gonna have to not only complete the assignments satisfactorily—you're gonna have to get *published* somehow. Newspaper, magazine, radio, TV—doesn't matter how. Show me some moxie!"

Maribeth was cowed. Maybe she should drop the class while there was still time....

First, she decided to call her English mentor, Mrs. Keller. "Miss-us Kay, the ... the ... teeeeeacher wants us to g-g-get on ra-dio or in the news-paper. That's haaard!"

"Well, yes! That would be hard for anybody, Maribeth. Don't drop the class yet, though. Let's talk more...."

Mrs. Keller came over to Maribeth's house that evening. With her she brought the yellow pages of the St. Louis phone book. "Let's find some nonprofit organization you could consider reporting about. They might be more willing to cooperate with you because you could get them some free advertising if you get an article published. The newspapers are always looking for well-written local human interest stories...."

One thing led to another. Maribeth passed her class with an A+ because she not only had her article published, she even appeared briefly on the local news broadcast as a direct result. She began to realize that she could combine her inborn talent for expressing herself in writing with her other gifts and inclinations, which she suspected had been given to her by God to be used for his glory.

Now, at the age of twenty-eight, Maribeth is living in her own specially equipped apartment, working part-time for an organization that provides free legal assistance to the disabled. She is still working on a college degree, one course at a time. In her "spare" time, she organizes denominational retreats for disabled Christian singles, an incredibly detail-encumbered task. The retreats are sponsored by a camp near St. Louis and are attended by young adults from all over the nation. Her administrative gift has come into its own, as well as her teaching gift, which is sometimes used in her secular job for writing manuals and organizing information for her employer's clients, but more often for her church work. She is in the process of writing up some of the "Best Retreats" material to be sent out to the folks on the singles' mailing list.

Her gift of mercy is evident in her writing. Her empathy is real because she knows her readers' pain firsthand. She is not handicapped in her ability to help others along the rocky path of life.

"I almost forget I'm disabled when I'm at the computer," Maribeth confided in a recent article for fellow singles. "Also when I'm worshipping God. You know, I'll have a perfect body when I get to heaven! In the meantime, I'm going to read, write, and rejoice."

Bedridden intercessor Also physically handicapped—but not in terms of her spiritual gifts—was a woman in London, England, who was cared for by her sister because she was bedridden. The following story, condensed here, is told by E.M. Bounds, Civil War chaplain, pastor, prolific writer, and himself an intercessor.[2]

In 1872, the famous evangelist Dwight L. Moody went to England to take a break from his demanding preaching schedule. His intention was to travel, listening and learning from *other* preachers. One Sunday, however, he did agree to preach in a London church. The spiritual atmosphere that day was so utterly dead that he began to question his decision to preach, especially because he was expected to preach again that evening. He had never had such a hard time preaching in his life.

That evening, when he faced the now-dreaded duty, he could hardly believe it was the same congregation. The pews were packed, the spiritual atmosphere was supercharged, and, most unexpected of all, five hundred people stood in response to an invitation to become Christians. Moody was incredulous. He re-issued the invitation, thinking that surely so many people couldn't be sincere. All five hundred were in earnest, and that night marked the beginning of a revival in that vicinity.

Later he found out that his "secret spiritual weapon" was the invalid sister of a woman who had attended the extraordinarily barren morning service. Upon her return home from morning worship, she had mentioned the preacher's name to her sister, who went pale with astonishment. "What? Mr. Moody from Chicago? I read about him some time ago in an American paper, and I have been praying to God to send him to London, and to our church. If I had known he was going to preach this morning I would have eaten no breakfast. I would have spent the whole time in prayer. Now, sister, go out of the room, lock the door, send me no dinner; no matter who comes, don't let them see me. I am going to spend the whole afternoon and evening in prayer."

She did, and God delighted to answer her! Quite likely the fact that she was an invalid was not a hindrance to her use of the gift of intercession. I wish we knew her name. God certainly does.

Not Backward in Gifts

Almost all of us know someone who has a family member with Down's syndrome. We're familiar with the distinctive physical and mental features of this disability. Most of us are also aware that people with Down's syndrome tend to have very affectionate and cheerful personalities, but their considerable limitations make them unable to live independently.

Are they passed by when God distributes spiritual gifts? I don't think so, provided that the individual has been raised in a home where Christ is named with respect and where his love is modeled.

I remember Kim, who was a "surprise baby" in more ways than one to her older parents. The only reason they could rally to the challenge of raising and caring for their last daughter, who would never be able to leave the nest as the others had, is because of their secure faith in God.

Kimmie knows she is loved. And she likes to make other people feel better when they are sad. Once at a church picnic, she tried to share her cup of soda with a toddler who was crying, petting his head and sobbing with him. She enjoys lugging the dirty laundry to the basement for her mother and takes delight in smoothing the folded piles when she returns the clean clothes to their owners. When visitors come to her house, she loves to greet them at the door. She keeps a close and friendly eye on them while they talk with her mother or father, being quick to take the cue that it is time for refreshments. She loves to carry a plate of cookies or the teapot to the coffee table for her mother and is solicitous if a guest drains his or her cup. She is, in short, helpful and hospitable, caring and merciful. What more could you ask?

Kimmie will never be a Scripture scholar. Kimmie will never deliver speeches or travel to foreign lands as a missionary. She will never have children and teach them their ABCs. But Kimmie will demonstrate the gifts that suit her: mercy, helps, and hospitality. She demonstrates them so purely that many of us, with our cluttered mental and emotional agendas, could take a lesson or two from her!

We all, limited in many ways, serve a God who knows how weak we are, and yet wants us to share in his kingdom work and has given us spiritual gifts so that we can be his arms and legs and mouthpieces on earth.

Ten

Gifts That Astound

Babsie Bleasdell, an energetic Catholic charismatic leader in Trinidad, tells a story in her recent book, *Refresh Your Life in the Spirit*[1] that illustrates a number of gifts in operation:

Babsie was giving a teaching at a prayer meeting. Suddenly, a woman in one of the chairs became violently ill. The sick woman was helped to another part of the hall, and some of the people stayed to tend her.

As Babsie continued to teach, seemingly unperturbed by the emergency situation, a third woman urged her to stop teaching and go to pray with the sick woman. Babsie insisted that the other people were capable of taking care of her and that her job was to continue speaking. But the third woman (whose urgings Babsie later realized were prophetic in nature) persisted until she cooperated to please her.

The sick woman's helpers had phoned for a doctor and were standing around her prone body, waiting for medical assistance to arrive. Babsie knelt down and began to pray with her.

"While I was praying with her," she reports, "I had a sudden feeling that she had died. Sweat covered her whole body, and she was as pale as death. I don't know if she really was clinically dead, but she sure looked it. I felt sure she was at least near death. Something seemed to roll up inside me, and I blurted, 'But you can't die. You're at a prayer meeting!'"

Babsie was given sudden and complete faith. She commanded, "In the name of Jesus, I speak life to this woman. Let the soul return to the body in Jesus' name!"

At those words, the waxen face of the woman became flushed. Babsie uttered the next words that occurred to her, "I impart life to you in Jesus' name. In Jesus' name, arise!" And the woman opened her eyes.

"How are you?"

"I feel all right."

"Would you like to get up?"

(I love her response. It gives a ring of authenticity to an account that might otherwise strain our credulity.) "Well, they sent for the doctor, and you know how doctors are when you send for them and they come and you are sitting up...." So Babsie left her there with a blessing, still lying down, but smiling and in perfect health.

Her account ends here. I presume she returned to the rest of the group to resume her teaching duty in a matter-of-fact way, probably with a nod of thanks to the persistent one who had goaded her into action a few minutes before.

Look at the gifts we see here: Babsie, who had been busy exercising her spiritual gift of teaching, had been interrupted by a prophetically gifted member of the prayer group who had a sense of urgency. Babsie herself didn't have any particular urgency until she started to pray. Then she experienced God's gift of faith for the occasion—enough faith to raise someone from the dead. (Gifts of healing and miracles seem to be given hand in glove with the gift of faith.)

What Is a Miracle?

I don't suppose anyone in Babsie's prayer group bothered to split hairs to categorize the outcome as either a *healing* from illness or a *miracle*—or both. What mattered to them was that their friend was smiling again and that God had manifested his power in their midst.

Christians spar about what constitutes a "true" healing or "verified" miracle. This can cause us to miss the point: We serve a mighty God who is interested in our welfare. The apostle Paul's references to miracles are almost casual (see, for example, Gal 3:5). In the Acts of the Apostles, great "signs and wonders" are mentioned without any effort to differentiate healing or deliverance from other kinds of miracles. Some miraculous events were even punitive—remember the deaths of Ananias and Sapphira (see Acts 5) and the blinding rebuke of Elymas the magician (see Acts 13:8-11), both of which also illustrate prophetic spiritual discernment.

Theologian Wayne Grudem defines a miracle as follows: "a less common kind of God's activity in which he arouses people's awe and wonder and bears witness to himself."[2] When miraculous events involve someone's active prayer, especially more than once, we may say that he or she possesses a spiritual gift of miracles.

The gift of miracles is listed in 1 Corinthians 12:10, immediately after the gifts of healing and faith. Although God is perfectly capable of performing healings and miracles "out of the blue," without human involvement, he has apparently given some individuals gifts that enable them to have their prayers answered in amazing ways. Such supernatural occurrences, tailor-made to the needs of the people affected, transcend natural explanations. Almost always, they occur before witnesses. Faith in God increases as a result of seeing a healing or other miracle event.

What Is Faith?

"Faith is being sure of what we hope for and certain of what we do not see" (Heb 11:1). Faith is fundamental to the Christian life, so frequently mentioned in Scripture that the spiritual gift of faith can be difficult to differentiate from the basic faith equipment of a Christian. It is listed both as a spiritual gift (see 1 Cor 12:9) and as one of the fruits of the Spirit (see Gal 5:22). How do you know if you have a spiritual *gift* of faith?

The gift of faith seems to be "super-added" to one's ordinary level of basic faith in God. It may rise up suddenly to accompany a startling miracle, or it may be steady and persevering over a long period of time. Remember Reville Johnson (chapter 8). Think of women you know—maybe you are one of them—who have unwavering faith that their non-Christian husbands will eventually join them at the throne of God. Think of women like Gladys Aylward, who, as an uneducated Cockney parlor maid, pursued her dream of becoming a missionary to China against all odds. Her gift of faith had many further opportunities to be exercised during her strenuous career. Her story, which was made into the movie *The Inn of the Sixth Happiness*,[3] proves that her desire came from God. (Incidentally, her story also illustrates a woman working to plant churches where no one had ever heard the gospel. Many would consider that to be the gift of apostle in action.)

Faith Multiplication

Sometimes it's the "everyday miracles" that increase our faith the most. For instance, when my husband and I were newlyweds, we were invited to dinner by a single friend who lived with three other Christian women, all college students. The invitation was quite spontaneous. Unfortunately, there really wasn't enough food for two extra people. A chicken dinner was already in the oven. A single chicken had been purchased and cut up: two drumsticks, two thighs, two breasts, two wings, and one bony back. Apologetically, the cook volunteered to forego her portion so that we guests could eat. When the oven timer rang, she opened the door and reached in with a potholder to pull out the pan. On it were *two extra drumsticks,* four altogether, nicely baked! "My favorite!" enthused the delighted cook.

It had never occurred to the cook to pray that her chicken pieces would multiply in the oven, but the faith of everyone in the apartment multiplied as a result!

Storm warning. Faith was increased in the hearts of a church youth group in Georgia 1983 when Priscilla Dunning prayed that a violent approaching storm would not wash away their sand sculpture. They had worked for hours modeling a prize-winning depiction of Golgotha on the ocean beach. But the judges from the youth convention hadn't completed their rounds yet. The clouds were alarmingly black, and sheets of rain coursed toward the shore across the ocean waves. Priss prayed aloud, "Lord, punch your hand through these clouds. Please let it rain everywhere *except* on this stretch of beach for at least two more hours, so that the judging can be completed." That's exactly how it happened. And all the teens knew Who had done it.

Batteries not included. Author Robert DeGrandis tells the following story:

> Late one evening two teenage sisters left a shopping mall and headed for their car. It was dark and silent in the near-empty parking facility, and they were nervous. When they opened the car doors two men jumped out at them from behind the car, shouting, "You're not going anywhere! You're going with us!" The girls screamed and locked themselves in the car. The driver turned on the ignition and nothing happened. She tried again. No response. The men tried the doors. The girls joined hands and the driver prayed, "Dear God, please give us a miracle!" She turned on the ignition again and the motor started. She shifted into gear and raced out of the parking lot, leaving the men behind.
>
> Safe at home, the girls told their father about the frightening experience. "I'm glad you're safe. That's the main thing. But don't stay out so late again." Then he reflected for an instant. "The car has never failed to start before. I'll check it out tomorrow." The next morning he raised the car's hood to examine the starter and saw something that raised gooseflesh on his arms: There was no battery![4]

Nothing is impossible for God.

Breath of Life

The same God who can make a car engine operate without a battery also can make a diseased heart healthy. Linda Horning is a stay-at-home mom in her early fifties who volunteers much of her time with Moms in Touch International, an interdenominational organization that encourages mothers of school-age children to band together to pray for their schools. She told me this dramatic healing story.

"In July, 1997, my family attended an interdenominational family camp with preaching, singing, and a good youth program. We go every year and we love it there.

"I had become friends with the head cook. One day I was having a late breakfast with her in the camp cafeteria. She introduced me to her friend from Ohio, a woman about my age. I was shocked to discover that this relatively young woman had been diagnosed with congestive heart failure. Her disease was so advanced that she had been recommended for a heart transplant. She had requested healing prayers in various Christian groups many times, to no avail.

"After we had finished eating and were standing to leave, the cook suddenly said, 'We've just gotta pray!' Most people had left the cafeteria by then.

"In general, I am comfortable praying for people and I usually do it with my eyes closed, touching the person lightly with my hands. This time, however, I began to feel that God wanted me to sort of *breathe* healing into her. That seemed a little weird, but I remembered that God had breathed life into Adam and that Jesus had once made blindness-healing mud using his own spittle, so maybe this was one of God's creative ideas. *I* certainly wouldn't have thought it up! I asked her permission and she said yes. I breathed gently and persistently into her mouth as I prayed silently.

"Suddenly, the woman *jumped* up and started exclaiming 'I'm *healed!* I can feel it! My heart feels different!' She screamed and cried and jumped up and down and ran around the table.

"She sure seemed to be healthy for the rest of camp, and later her Ohio doctors verified the healing. They canceled their request for a heart transplant. I don't see the cook between camp meetings, but this summer [1998] I could hardly wait to ask about her friend. 'Is she still healed a year later?'

"'Yes, she is. Isn't God good?'"

Plural Gifts

Many Bible commentators point out that Paul's references to gifts of healing and miracles are plural. This fits with firsthand observation; Christians often have identifiable "specialties" such as emotional ("inner") healing or healing from specific physical ailments. Here again, glorious variety is God's hallmark. Better not box up *this* gift!

The healed as healers. Often, someone who has received God's healing can pray for others to be healed of the same ailment. I know of a documented case of a teenage girl who was healed of dyslexia and who now prays—successfully and frequently—for others in churches near her home. She seems to be a dyslexia specialist!

Teacher to student. Karen Burton Mains tells the story of a close friend who was a music teacher in a private inner-city school where there were many emotionally troubled children. She had "yielded herself to the Holy Spirit and had begun to grope with the meaning of the gifts of healing, [seeking] wisdom as to how to minister in her profession."

Karen writes that "every morning she was assigned to monitor the cafeteria before school. She took her Bible and spent that half-hour in prayer, asking God to fill the troubled school with His presence. Private lessons gave her close physical contact with students. Laying her hands casually on some troubled child, she would instruct music, all the while praying that God would use her as a channel for His healing, that He would fill the disordered personality with love and restore any chemical imbalance."

She chose performance music that would "stimulate religious thinking," with words often taken straight from Scripture. As the year progressed, she saw some hopeful signs. She also encountered spiritual resistance in the form of pressure from the school administration. "At the end of the year, wearied and a little worn from the efforts, she was rewarded by the words of the special education teacher who said that in 'all of her years of teaching she had never had so much success with so many difficult cases.' Little did the other teacher realize the hours of prayer ... that had aided her."[5]

Teamwork. We are knit together as members of the body of Christ. Just as conversions so often result from the invisible collaborative efforts of many Christians, so too healings can come through more than one individual. They can also be progressive rather than sudden. These aspects were highlighted for me as I started to write this chapter.

On Labor Day weekend, our office carpets had been cleaned with some kind of perfumed shampoo. Our editorial assistant, Christa, had begun to suffer from migraines when she was in college, and perfumes seemed to be one of the "triggers." Christa tried everything, but the lingering scent caused debilitating headaches day after day.

As I thought of her in my morning prayer one day, I felt motivated by Jesus' compassion to offer to pray with her several times a week, although I have never felt I had much of a gift of healing.

Interesting to both of us, my brief but regular prayers did

have some effect. Christa felt heat when I touched her forehead, sometimes a spreading warmth down her neck (I felt nothing), and the headaches "backed off" each time. But they didn't go away.

Then one weekend, Christa received prayer twice from her husband and an older Christian relative who often prayed with people. Those prayers, which involved some repentance for college exposure to non-Christian religions and some deliverance from evil spirits, helped noticeably. The headaches are continuing to disappear as she prays for herself and asks God for further help.

Listen to the Healer

A woman who has the gift of healing needs to learn a vital truth and hold it closely: *Always, always listen to God.* The most important element of any healing is our personal relationship with him. He is the Healer; we are his servants. He loves each individual uniquely and wants us to administer his healing touch appropriately. Sometimes God wants us to refrain from praying directly for healing or to be ready to do something else instead.

For example, one day after church a woman asked me to lay hands on her to pray "for her hearing loss." Although I am usually quick with words, I found that I could not form the words of a prayer for that request. My mind was blank. I considered the matter, then felt that the Holy Spirit gave me an idea for a slightly different prayer—to pray against her fear of going deaf. Effectiveness depends upon obedience, and I did have both the faith and the words to pray the second prayer effectively.

The importance of listening to God is underlined by Agnes Sanford, one of the women who pioneered the mid-twentieth-century renewal of interest in the gift of healing. When her husband, a pastor who was past seventy, was in rapidly declining health, she had asked God whether or not to pray for his healing. She knew that he might be nearing the end of his allotted time on earth. Although she didn't want to lose him, she herself felt peace about not praying for his healing. However, his loyal parishioners "did not consider these matters, but prayed definitely for healing. I counsel people to ask guidance before leaping into healing prayers, but few pay any attention. Ted did make a [temporary] recovery, but indeed and truly he was not himself."[6]

With healing, as with any gift, we must remember that we belong to God. We do not call the shots. He does.

Deliver Us From Evil

As we saw with Christa, healing and deliverance from evil spirits can come hand in hand. That connection sometimes serves to bring the gift of deliverance to our attention in the first place.

Julia was still in college when she began to feel drawn to pray with fellow students in her campus chapel's Wednesday evening Bible study/prayer group. They welcomed her prayers. Some of them claimed they were healed of colds or backaches.

On a particular Wednesday, one of the student leaders, Brad, brought a guest. He introduced him to the group as "Norm from my dorm." After the chuckles about the accidental rhyme had died down, Norm, who seemed to have laryngitis, said he was glad to have been invited. Julia felt compassion for Norm as he struggled to talk.

At the end of the meeting, she introduced herself to him and volunteered to pray for his voice to come back. Norm looked a little surprised, which Julia attributed to his unfamiliarity with such a concept. Brad told him, "It can't hurt, Norm. Seems like you've had this bug too long already."

Brad, Julia, and Norm stayed after the others had left. "This'll just take a minute," Julia said, arranging three plastic chairs to face each other. "Let's pray, Norm."

No sooner had she begun to pray that Norm's laryngitis would be healed than she stopped cold—Norm was *growling!* His eyes looked weird. She and Brad were stunned.

Julia says she somehow knew what "category of thing" to do—that it had something to do with Satan. The only Scripture that came to her mind was James 4:7 (RSV), "Resist the devil and he will flee from you." So she said those words from memory several times, finally changing them into her own prayer, "So, Satan, I resist you in the name of Jesus!" The growling stopped and Norm looked around, embarrassed.

The three of them didn't know what to do after that, so they went home, with a tacit agreement to suspend judgment on the experience.

After that event, Julia "kept her feelers up," as she puts it, for more information about this sort of thing. She wanted to know what the Bible said about evil spirits and what other Christians had learned. She was pretty sure what the growling meant, but she didn't know what to do about it. She worried that it would happen again sometime in her prayers for healing.

The next time it happened without growling. During prayer for personal needs, a college freshman named Camille said to Julie, "I just feel like something inside me wants to curse at you." Again, Julia stopped the prayer session. This time, she made an appointment with her pastor for herself and Camille. Without fanfare, the two of them cast an evil spirit out of her and surrounded her with prayer and good advice. Camille said she felt "lighter" afterward and she never felt that "cursing thing" rise up in her again.

After college, Julia moved to another town and joined a new church. She continued to learn bits and pieces about how Satan afflicts human lives and how she could pray against his work. After reading a book about spiritual gifts, she decided that she had a gift of deliverance. She was *not* thrilled. However, she was willing to use it if God would help her. She did seem to have the gift of discernment of spirits, which helped very much as she formulated appropriate prayers for people.

Twice Julia went with organized groups on short-term mission trips, once to Haiti and once to Nicaragua. There she had opportunities to see others using the same gift, often in connection with evangelistic outreach. In those cultures, the contrast between darkness and light seemed to be so much greater.

Eventually, Julia was appointed as a "prayer minister" after going to pursue extra training at an evangelical seminary. She uses the gift in the context of helping the pastor to counsel and pray with individuals in the church.

"Deliverance is not my favorite gift, frankly," she confesses. "I prefer to use the gift of healing, although I actually see more successes in the area of deliverance. I really enjoy using my gifts of hospitality and my musical abilities. However, I want to keep growing, keep close to Jesus, and keep obeying his Holy Spirit. My personal integrity is so important, and I know it. Somebody has to stand firm against the enemy, not just on the mission field, but even here in the middle-class suburbs where I live. I'll do it—for the Lord and with his help!"

Healing, miracles, and deliverance, all dependent upon a gift of faith, also depend entirely upon God's sovereignty. Successes are not guaranteed. Even the foremost healer, Jesus, when he was at the Pool of Bethesda, where faith was intense, healed only one man. He modeled responsiveness to his sovereign

Father, who has compassion on us but who knows absolutely the best way to administer healing in our lives.

How grateful we can be that he not only healed the sick, multiplied the loaves and fish, and raised the dead when he walked the earth, but that he still does it today—through members of his church who are gifted and obedient.

Eleven

Does God Sing Soprano?

God sings all the parts: soprano, alto, tenor, and bass, too, joined with the music of the spheres. In this chapter I want to show you some more examples of how women speak on God's behalf.

This chapter is about the supernatural gifts of tongues, interpretation of tongues, and prophecy. The gift of tongues includes the ability to sing in tongues (or to follow a spontaneously inspired tune as you sing in your native language or play an instrument during worship). The gift of prophecy includes spoken words, inspired visions, and dreams.

O for a Thousand Tongues to Sing

The gift of tongues, or *glossolalia,* gets more than its share of attention and is frequently a "hot button" in discussions between Christians of differing backgrounds. I want to be as straightforward as possible about the gift.

As a Presbyterian, I remember this from the Westminster Shorter Catechism: "The chief end of man is to glorify God and to *enjoy him forever.*" I can pray in tongues seriously—even desperately—but I often pray in tongues because my spirit is bubbling over with joy. Like a child, I'm enjoying my relationship with my Father, God.[1]

When I speak in tongues, my spirit, united with God's Spirit, is free to express itself in a language that I have never studied or heard spoken. Because I can't understand my words, my mind is free to think simultaneous prayers in my native English. And although I have learned some French, Spanish, and Russian, my prayer languages bear little resemblance to those languages. Classical Pentecostal preacher Harold Horton has declared that "the linguistic skill of man is no more employed in speaking with tongues than the surgical skill of man was employed when, at Peter's word, 'Rise and walk,' the lame man instantly arose."[2]

Despite the seemingly meaningless words we vocalize, those of us who speak in tongues know that we are praying effectively. Whether worshipping or interceding for others, alone or in a group, silently or loudly or perhaps with song, we are confident that we are praying according to the inspiration of God's Spirit.

Some have experienced supernatural protection when they prayed in tongues. One of my friends, who has struggled with lifelong depression, told me that once she was seriously considering suicide. But she remembered, "When you don't know what to pray, you can always pray in tongues." She did, and the temptation lifted. She felt that God saved her life through her use of the gift of tongues.

Some insist that it is one of the "least" of the gifts because it is listed last in 1 Corinthians 12:10. (Does that make love the least of the Christian graces because Paul lists it after faith and hope in 1 Corinthians 13:13?) Far from being unimportant, the gift of tongues was part of the "standard-issue equipment" for early Christians. It remains common to this day, each recipient praying in a language distinct from others', although many dynamic Christians do not have this gift.

Even those whose church doctrine stands firmly against the use of speaking in tongues can accept the following true story.

"Speak Out!"

Linda Horning, mentioned in chapter 10, told me that before she was married, the gift of tongues was new to her, so new, in fact, that she still had doubts about it. "I didn't doubt the gift *per se* but I wasn't so sure what I was doing was the 'real thing.'"

One day, a bigger skeptic was visiting from Ireland, and he questioned her about the gift of tongues. He admitted that he couldn't bring himself to pray out loud even in English. He felt terribly self-conscious and inhibited about letting others overhear his prayers.

Linda explained conventional wisdom about the two subjects, reading some psalms about praying aloud in general and the passages from 1 Corinthians about the gift of tongues in particular. She could tell this wasn't enough, so she suggested that they just pray together quietly for a while. She wanted to give him "practice" praying aloud in English in the hearing of another person.

At first, he spoke out quietly but audibly, and Linda was encouraged. She prayed out loud too, eventually switching to pray in her prayer language, which she had mentioned beforehand that she might do. Suddenly, he fell silent.

"How's it going? Feeling a bit more comfortable with praying out loud? I just wondered because you stopped," Linda said, looking up.

He was sitting there with a completely dumbstruck look on his face.

"You have been praying in perfect Gaelic," he whispered. "And you have been saying to me, over and over, in Gaelic, 'Speak out!'"

Now it was Linda's turn to be dumbstruck!

"It's true," he said. "In Ireland, we all learn Gaelic in school, although it is a dead language. But the phrase is [and he said it in Gaelic; Linda has since forgotten it, although she says she remembered it for years]. It was the main point of your message in Gaelic."

Needless to say, not one but two doubters were convinced of the far-reaching possibilities in God's kingdom.

O for a Thousand Interpretations

Such an experience of direct translation of an utterance in tongues is rare, and most people's prayer languages will remain unidentified. This is the reason for the gift of interpretation of tongues.

On occasion, a person with the gift of tongues feels inspired to speak out loud in a gathering of Christians where it is acceptable to do so. Such public utterances in tongues need to be interpreted by someone with the gift of interpretation of tongues, which could be the same person. This raises the pronouncement closer to the level of a prophetic declaration (see 1 Cor 14:13 and 1 Cor 12:10).

Interpretation is not the same as translation, but rather an expression of the *sense* of the message. An interpretation provides something for our intellects to grasp, giving meaning to an otherwise meaningless jumble of syllables, "much the same as Hammerstein might supply the words to a score that Rodgers has written."[3]

Why not just deliver straight prophecy if interpretation of tongues is so similar? Primarily because the purpose of the messages is different. Messages in tongues usually express prayerful exultation to God, not so much prophetic "forthtelling." Both build up the body of Christ.

Besides, there is no doubt about it: An utterance in tongues arrests the attention of the hearers. God wants our attention before we doze off in prayer meetings!

To Hear the Father's Voice

I have saved the gift of prophecy for last because it is interwoven with all of the other gifts and since, in its most elementary definition, the prophetic gift is simply *hearing God's voice.* I realize that this is a broader definition than many commentators prefer. However, I believe that prayer is two-way communication and that God wants us to be able to hear him for ourselves and for each other. It seems artificial to consider only God's more complete communications, such as biblical prophetic words, to be "true prophecy." Far from dying out in the first century, I believe that prophecy is as alive and well today as is our living relationship with God.

"The fact is that no one can even become a true Christian without receiving a direct personal revelation from the Holy Spirit. In other words, no one comes to Jesus to be saved without 'hearing' from God. In this most basic sense, all Christians have experienced a form of prophecy."[4]

Prophets aren't an exclusive bunch. Paul writes, "Follow the way of love and eagerly desire spiritual gifts, especially the gift of prophecy" (1 Cor 14:1). Moses laments, "I wish that all the Lord's people were prophets" (Num 11:29). Sometimes "all" the people in a church prophesied (see 1 Cor 14:24, 31). Philip had four daughters, all of whom prophesied (see Acts 21:9).

"Speak, Lord. Your servant is listening" (see 1 Sam 3:10) should be our daily request. Whatever our gifts—including service-oriented gifts such as mercy, helps, hospitality, and service—we risk merely "doing good things" in our own strength if we don't ask often for clear direction. Remember Grace Bailey in chapter two? She was doing ordinary work, washing the dishes, when she felt God's "nudge" to get in the car and drive. Once she was underway, the second nudge came, "See that woman at the bus stop. Offer her a ride." That simple act of mercy might have been adequate reason for God's leading. As it turned out, it led to a remarkable harvest for the kingdom of God. But it started with hearing God's whisper. That's the gift of prophecy in its most basic form. Grace didn't preach in words, she *acted* out of what she heard. She showed a stranger that God cared, that God wanted to take initiative in her life. She represented God by her actions.

Modern-day prophets "forthtell" such aspects of God's nature more than they foretell the future. At different times, and depending upon the other qualifications of the messenger, prophets may express words of inspiration and edification, encouragement, reproof, teaching, and guidance (usually less directive and more indicative: "such and such is coming"). (See examples in Acts 15:32; 1 Cor 14:3-4, 24; 1 Cor 2:6-13.) A prophetic intercessor may know just when to pray for certain people.

"Thus saith the Lord" is *not* the required mode of delivery for a prophetic word—simple language suffices. Often the prophetic sense is woven into a prophetic, faith-building intercessory prayer or a simple one-on-one encouragement. Sometimes a "word" is first seen in vision form, or as a dream, in which cases it needs an interpretation much as the gift of tongues does. Sometimes a person finds a particular beginning (or ending) phrase coming to mind, and the rest of the word follows. Usually the prophetic sense comes as a simple mental impression, "just knowing with your knower." All forms of prophecy remain subject to the discernment of the hearers, whose corporate sanctified common sense is a great safeguard against falsehood and the taint of sinful motives or wishful thinking.

Chasing the Call

When Jackie Pullinger was twenty, she felt a strong pull from her native England to the mission field. She investigated every possible avenue of service, only to be denied. Then one day, she had a dream. In it, her family was clustered around the dining room table scrutinizing a map. She writes, "In the middle of the different colored countries was a pink one. It said 'Hong Kong.'" Afterward, she wrote to the government of Hong Kong requesting a teaching job in that country—but she was denied.

Desperate for further guidance, Jackie happened to be in a tiny, empty village church. While she was praying there, she saw a vision in which a woman was "holding out her arms beseechingly as on a refugee poster." Then words moved past like a television credit: "What can you give us?" This made her think long and hard about her purpose in pursuing a missionary appointment to Hong Kong.

Then a friend invited her to a prayer meeting. Nervous, because apparently the people were going to use "spiritual gifts," Jackie sat by the door in case she needed to make a quick getaway. She reports,

> I was not sure what to expect and I thought maybe someone would prophesy in a loud voice, "You'll meet a man who'll

> give you a ticket for such and such a country on such and such a date" and that would be God's way of answering me.
>
> [But] the meeting was orderly and calm with normal prayers and songs.... No booming voice.
>
> Then it came.... Someone was speaking quite quietly and I was completely sure that it was meant for me: "Go, trust me, and I will lead you. I will instruct you and teach you in the way which you shall go; I will guide you with my eye." There it was, what he had been saying all along, but now it was underlined.

With the help of a trusted advisor, she decided to book passage on a boat going in the direction of Hong Kong and to pray to know when to get off.

The rest, as they say, is history. Jackie did disembark at Hong Kong, and she began to befriend the "low-lifes" within the "Walled City," a reeking, drug- and crime-infested few acres where hundreds of thousands of desperate people lived. Jackie is still, to this day, bringing hundreds of desperate men and women to new life. It was through the gift of prophecy that God revealed his direction for her life—in stages.[5]

Closer to home. It is a safeguard for us that God's guidance comes to us most often through more than one person. Ché Ahn, Korean-American pastor of the large Harvest Rock Church in Pasadena, California, tells how two prophetic words, both offered by trusted women, showed him whom to hire as his church administrator.

> We desperately needed to hire a full-time administrator.... I had no clue how to begin looking for the right person who had both the appropriate spiritual and natural skills.
>
> ... My wife [Sue] received an open vision from heaven. It

> was a clear visual picture, almost like a daydream, that appeared real ... (see Acts 10:11). She saw Jeff Wright, the brother of Rick Wright [Ahn's associate pastor] walking around Mott auditorium [their meeting place] holding a clipboard in his hand. She knew immediately that Jeff was to be our administrator.
>
> A few months earlier, Rick's wife, Pam, had submitted a prophetic word to me that Sue had never heard. Pam said she sensed that one day Jeff was to join our staff.

Unbeknownst to Sue, Pam, or Ché, Jeff himself had received a prophetic word twelve years earlier that he would use his administrative gifts in a Christian ministry position. No position had ever opened, so he had served in secular jobs, all the while longing to be able to serve in a church. Now he serves at Harvest Rock Church, and, according to Ché, has been "the best administrative pastor I have ever known on any staff. It simply proves that if we will follow the Lord's prompting, each of us has an equal opportunity continually to step into the best 'fit' for His purposes and our needs."[6]

Graham Cooke writes, "Prophetic ministry is concerned with the church, and it is concerned with the direction we take, as well as who will lead and how we will get to our destination. Prophetic ministry brings God's perspective, releases vision and calling and undermines your enemy. It is concerned with the church fulfilling its call."[7] In these days of revived interest in the activity of the Holy Spirit, both men and women who have prophetic gifts should use them responsibly and generously.

To avoid abusing the privilege of speaking on God's behalf, we must remember the dual safeguards of openness to others' correction and basic purity of character. The extra potential power and authority of certain spiritual gifts requires, as the next chapter will make clear, extra personal integrity.

Twelve

Coming of Age

The downstairs mantel clock struck 4:00 A.M. Ellie was already awake, groping for her glasses on the bedside table. Not that they did her much good these days—the print in her Bible was small, and she hadn't scheduled that cataract surgery yet.

Shuffling into her slippers, her mind flashed back to forty-five years earlier. Same bed, same room, same time of night—but a baby had been crying across the hall for another feeding.

Now she was alone. Her "baby" had almost-grown babies of his own, and her husband had been gone for a decade. Four o'clock in the morning was *her* feeding time—time to feed on the Word of God and then turn to feed many others through her intercessory prayer. It was the best hour of the twenty-four in her long, lonely days.

Ellie had loved him—Jesus, that is—since she was a girl in North Carolina. Mama and Papa had loved him too. Jesus made everything right.

"It's true," she thought. "Life has seasons. Especially for a woman, maybe. I've had an easier lot than some of my friends, but I've had to move through so many seasons to get to where I am right now.

"First I was young. Giddy, Mama used to say. I had so much energy. And I loved to sing. Sure can't sing anymore, just croak.

I loved life, and I was sure everyone should love me. (I had some disappointments coming!) I went off to church three times a week because I loved to sing, because I loved being with other people, and, well, because everyone else did it."

Ellie settled into her big brown chair and hoisted the footrest. Her knobby fingers smoothed the leather cover of her Bible.

"Church is where I met Jesus. What a Savior! At some point I decided to read the Bible from cover to cover. I've never gotten tired of reading it.

"I remember when I wanted to be a lady preacher! Of all things! I had so much to say. That idea never led anywhere, especially after I met Ralph. Still, I wanted to make a difference in people's lives. I tried everything: organizing church women to help in the war effort, helping out at church every chance I got, taking care of sick neighbors. Once I even handed out tracts at the bus station."

She glanced at her humble room with its slipcovered furniture. "When Chase was born and Mama had to come live with me, I felt more confined, but I kept a neat house and liked to invite people over.

"After an evangelist came through town, Pastor Adkins started the Tuesday healing service. That suited me. I loved to pray for the folks who came, even the ones who came week after week and never 'got their healing.' Almost every week, Ralph stayed home with Chase, and I was free to go. I thought I'd found my 'true calling.' Wonderful days, those were!

"But before long, the seasons changed. Pastor Adkins moved to a different church, and Mama became bedridden. I couldn't have attended evening services even if they were still being held—which they weren't. But, looking back, I think that's when I finally began to really grow up. I was a grown woman, of course, but I had never had to sacrifice so much. Life sort of does things to you. That's when I memorized Galatians 5, the fruit of the Spirit. 'The fruit of the Spirit is love, joy, peace, long-suffering, gentleness, goodness, faith, meekness, temperance: against such there is no law.'

"It's been real good to have known those verses. I stopped thinking so much about doing things. I started thinking about the character qualities I wanted to pass on to my son."

Ellie opened her Bible to Galatians 5 and began to trace the familiar words with her fingertip. Next thing she knew, she was praying for her current pastor and his family, for her son's family, and for the list of missionaries she kept inside the front cover. The hours until dawn passed quickly.

Sweet Love

As Ellie has come to realize, a woman's life has many twists and turns. For a Christian woman, maturity of character counts much more than our record of activities.

First Corinthians 13 tells us that the spiritual gifts—even highly developed gifts—are worth nothing without love. Love is not a spiritual gift; love is God himself (see 1 Jn 4:16), and his Spirit of love dwells in us. God's measuring stick for our lives is based on our response to his love, not on the exercise of our spiritual gifts. The fruit of the Spirit comes to increased maturity as we stay close to our Savior.

Yes, it's the love that will last, not the spiritual gifts. In fact, when we get to heaven, our gifts will be swallowed up in the Whole of which they are now but a partial expression. What endears us to our Savior is our humble willingness to let him transform us into his likeness, not the high-profile ministries in which we have engaged.

"It is not necessary to be a *splashy* disciple to be a *special* disciple.... If you are quiet or shy, when you get to heaven you might want to take the opportunity to look up Rufus' mother [see Rom 16:13], Julia, and Nereus's sister [see Rom 16:15]. After all, they are examples of unassuming disciples whom the great, energetic, dynamic apostle Paul refused to overlook. He needed them for good balance, and so does the church."[1]

Ellie may well be performing the most valuable service of all her life in her "declining years." Andrew Murray would say so: "God seeks intercessors. He looks to see if the Church is training the great army of aged men and women, whose time of outward work is past, but who can strengthen the army of the 'elect, which cry day and night unto Him'" (Lk 18:7).[2]

Fountain of life. "I've discovered, to my delight, that spiritual gifts don't age," says Jill Briscoe, quoted in *Today's Christian Woman.*[3] Whatever spiritual gifts God has given you, you will keep until your last breath. Instead of becoming old with the passage of time, gifts seem to become newer all the time. We discover new aspects of our gifts.

An example: I have a gift of prophecy. I "hear" God's thoughts in my mind. Most often, prophecy blends with my gift of exhortation to enable me to "hit the nail right on the head" when I counsel or mentor women informally. Sometimes I find mental impressions coming to my attention (I wouldn't always call them "visions"), and they help me pray. Recently, I have begun to notice two new aspects to this gift: I have had occasional prophetic dreams and, more unique than that, in intercession and worship my hands have become active in what I can only call "prophetic gesture." They seem to move at the behest of a heavenly choreographer. Like an interpreter for the deaf, my gestures express the meaning of my prayers. It's delightfully new but familiar at the same time. I reflect, "So *that's* what my hands have always been wanting to do!"

OK to covet. "Eagerly desire [or "covet" (KJV)] the greater gifts" (1 Cor 12:31). Go after more! Don't sit in your pew waiting for a gift-laden angel to show up. Don't wait for your circumstances to change before you start seeking. Think about the church in Corinth to which Paul addressed these words: a messed-up bunch to be sure. Yet he wanted them to pursue the spiritual gifts even *before* they got themselves all squared away.

The earlier in life we become Christians and discover our spiritual gifts, the better. But what if you feel you have "wasted" years of your Christian life in a type of work mismatched to your gifts? Besides the fact that nothing is ever wasted in God's economy, it's never too late to unwrap your spiritual gifts and put them to work. Both gifts and fruit, although developed through our life seasons, are not strictly seasonal.

The Proof of the Pudding Is in the Eating

Keep experimenting with your spiritual gifts through all the seasons of your life as opportunities arise and your circumstances change.

Remember the "eureka" principle in chapter one? Pay attention to what excites you. What spiritual gift are you using? When you use this gift, do you feel freer, more alive, more in tune with God's will for your life?

"Don't be too easily convinced that God really wants you to do all sorts of work you needn't do," C.S. Lewis wrote from England to an American woman. "Remember that a belief in the virtues of doing for doing's sake is characteristically feminine, characteristically American, and characteristically modern."[4]

What if you are a young mother and, by default, find yourself slotted into the church nursery rotation? Such duty may well suit you. But perhaps at this stage of your homebound life, starved as you may be for adult contact, you really need to be in the church service, adult Sunday school, or coffee hour just to maintain your week-to-week sanity. Even if your church is too small to "let you off the hook," just recognizing why you're chafing under the duty may help you to better adjust to it.

Sink or swim. What if you falter or fail? You *thought* you knew what God wanted you to do and you *thought* you knew what your gifts are. But everything has collapsed. Listen to these words of wisdom:

> Our attempts at ministry do not always "work." In human terms not everything "worked" for Jesus. He ended up on a cross.... To be a follower of The Way, as the early Christians were called, is to live with the possibility that when our gifts are used for the common good, we may find ourselves in a suffering servant role. We may find ourselves on streets that are not safe, in situations that are not secure and comfortable, in homes that are not peaceful and at bedsides of despair.[5]

From 1888 until her death in 1928, I. Lilias Trotter was a missionary to North Africa. In England, she had been a close friend of the painter John Ruskin. She spurned a budding career as an artist to bury her talents in the desert, convinced beyond doubt that she had been called as a missionary. Nothing made her happier than to go out into the countryside among the people she loved. "Lilly," as the Arab Muslim women called her, prayed ceaselessly for the people of this region, guided by dreams and visions, although not often by tangible signs of success.

Her first years were "five years of unmitigated anguish," according to a friend. She was painfully conscious of spiritual warfare. The only conversions she witnessed were deathbed conversions. She wrote and illustrated a series of inexpensive pamphlets and one book, *Parables of the Cross*, which is out of print. Today, despite her forty-year sacrifice, the church remains invisible in North Africa. In earthly terms, I. Lilias Trotter had nothing to show for her lifework.

God views "failure" in a different light. Apparent defeat doesn't necessarily mean that you've misread your gifts. Your true successes are recorded in heaven. Your seeming defeats could be merely part of the constant testing to which we are subjected (see James 1).

Not surprisingly, our areas of giftedness often attract enemy target practice. Consider this observation from Joyce K. Ellis, author of *The 500 Hats of a Modern-Day Woman:*

> I believe that one of my spiritual gifts is faith. I have a keen vision and tenacious confidence in God's ability to do impossible things, yet one of my greatest areas of weakness is worry. My former boss has the gift of discernment and the ability to speak truth in a confusing situation, yet she admits that her greatest struggle is fear of what others will think of her if she speaks the truth. Another woman has the gift of hospitality yet battles busyness, procrastination, and pride issues that often keep her from opening her home to others.[6]

"Sandpaper ministry." Pundits tell us that the seasons of our lives, particularly the seasons of buffeting, can either "make us better, or make us bitter." We find particular challenges in our relationships with fellow believers and family members.

Perhaps you and your husband experience friction in your home, possibly in part because you have differing gifts. Or if you have a similar gift, say leadership, it can be hard to coexist in the same household. You rub against each other's rough edges. Your appreciation for each other's distinct qualities can be dulled by aggravation.

In Philippians 4:2-3, we read of two women in the early church who had had a big quarrel with each other. Euodia and Syntyche were energetic workers in their church. Perhaps it was their enthusiastic use of their spiritual gifts that set off their quarrel. Paul, who had quarreled with Barnabas and could understand how two passionate and gifted Christians could disagree, urged them to reconcile. The result of the sandpaper ministry is smoothing.

Maintaining our unity with fellow believers is part of maintaining our relationship with Jesus, our Source of love and life (see Jn 14:6). The closer we are to him, the more effectiveness we enjoy in our use of spiritual gifts.

The dressing room. Picture yourself at your preferred department store, heading into the dressing room with a pile of prospective clothing purchases over your arm. You try everything on to see what fits. You turn before the mirror, perhaps stepping out to ask your shopping companion what she thinks. You evaluate the desirability of each piece to your wardrobe. You remember what you have learned about certain styles and fabrics, avoiding the ones you have found unsuitable in the past.

Finally, you make your selections and head to the cash register, ready to take your new garments home. They may be worn for a season or two, then discarded. Or they may become old favorites, worn even when your teenager says, "Mom! Are you still wearing that old thing?"

Apply this image to the seasons of your life and your spiritual gifts. Some gifts will seem to fit and some just won't. Of those that do fit, you may use one for a season—or for a lifetime. With God's help, you evaluate their usefulness from time to time. You mix and match them with other gifts. You may alter them to fit better. You may share them with your daughter who is about your size. You learn what suits you best by God-guided experimentation.

I have a gift but they won't let me use it! Is this your outcry, "they" being church bureaucracies, non-Christian husbands, or the frustrations of inaccessible resources? You know what your gifts are, but people or circumstances seem to conspire against your use of them?

Even when your gifts are "on hold," there's always a way to use them, if not in this season, then in the next. You can't manage them as you would manage a business. Hang on faithfully. Pray for renewed opportunities. Be flexible. Grow in patient endurance. Chances are God will surprise you, moving you into yet-unexplored realms of service, stirring up gifts you didn't even know you had.

If a coal falls out of the fireplace, it grows cold. Don't leave the church, even if you feel that you aren't "being fed," or that your particular gifts are not being appreciated. You may need to find a new church (if possible and if God seems to say OK) but don't become a Lone Ranger. Believers belong in the body.

If you are frustrated specifically because "they" don't want a woman to use her gifts, ask God for a creative way to do it. Elisabeth Elliot reminds us,

> "All members do not have the same function" [Rom 12:4]. There is nothing interchangeable about Christians. God has given gifts that *differ.* They differ *according to the grace given to us.* You and I, whether we are men or women, have nothing to do with the choice of the gift. We have everything to do with the use of the gift.
>
> There have surely been tens of thousands of anonymous women who have done what God sent them to do—and they've done it without the tub-thumping of modern egalitarian movements. They had a place and they knew they had it because Scripture says they have.[7]

As we move through the seasons of our lives, the demands of our jobs or our families may threaten to supersede all forms of Christian service. But we need to rise to the challenges of changing circumstances and seasons. Our fruit won't grow without the full round of seasons. And it may rot on our trees if we don't pluck it to share it with others—expressing God's love through as many of our spiritual gifts as we can.

Prayer for You

As you hold this book in your hand, I want to pray for you using Paul's prayer for the Ephesians. Please pray in turn for many others who are reading this book:

> I ask ... the God of our Master, Jesus Christ, the God of glory—to make you intelligent and discerning in knowing

him personally, your eyes focused and clear, so that you can see exactly what it is he is calling you to do, grasp the immensity of this glorious way of life he has for Christians, oh, the utter extravagance of his work in us who trust him—endless energy, boundless strength!

EPHESIANS 1:17-19, THE MESSAGE

Appendix

*Spiritual Gifts Survey for Women**

Read the definition for each gift. Underneath each definition you will find more detailed information about that gift, which you should read in light of the definition itself. The plus sign indicates positive traits. The minus sign indicates negative traits that can appear if you use your gift by your own strength instead of by the power of the Holy Spirit. Remember that no definition can perfectly capture the unlimited possibilities of God's creativity. Additional information about each gift and examples of the gifts being used by women can be found in the text of this book.

Think about the way you really are (including past experiences and what people have told you they see in you), not the way you would like to be. Mark the qualities you have seen in yourself. You will mark the most qualities for the gifts you possess in greatest measure. As you grow in your Christian life, you will gather more evidence of your spiritual gifts in action.

* Adapted from Priscilla B. Dunning, ©1998.

The Gift of Administration

A woman with the gift of administration has the ability to grasp a broad vision for a Christian organization or an event, to define goals, and to organize people to achieve them. She can see past traditional systems to devise solutions for problems. She has good mid- to long-range perspective and longer-term commitments are comfortable to her.

How many of these apply to you?

+

I tend to—

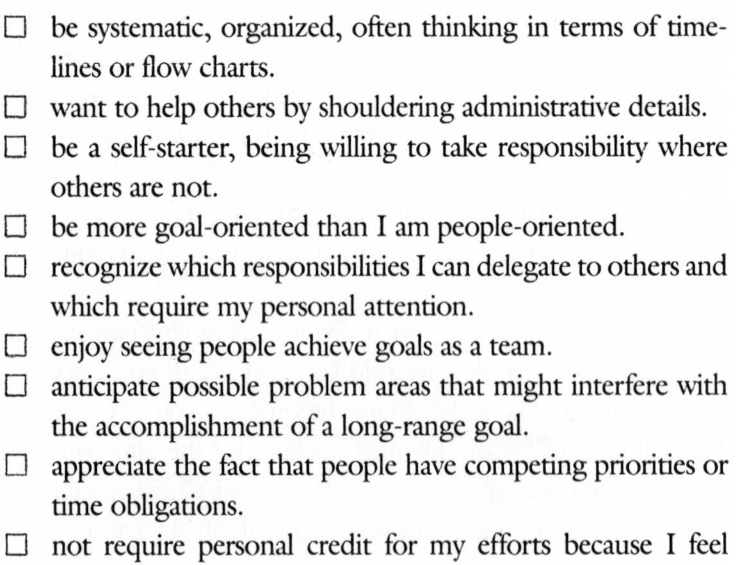

- ☐ be systematic, organized, often thinking in terms of timelines or flow charts.
- ☐ want to help others by shouldering administrative details.
- ☐ be a self-starter, being willing to take responsibility where others are not.
- ☐ be more goal-oriented than I am people-oriented.
- ☐ recognize which responsibilities I can delegate to others and which require my personal attention.
- ☐ enjoy seeing people achieve goals as a team.
- ☐ anticipate possible problem areas that might interfere with the accomplishment of a long-range goal.
- ☐ appreciate the fact that people have competing priorities or time obligations.
- ☐ not require personal credit for my efforts because I feel repaid by the successful completion of the project.

—

- ☐ rely too much on my natural organizational ability or my skills from the secular workplace and too little on the Holy Spirit.

☐ sometimes begin to see a project as mine, not the Lord's.
☐ become dictatorial, monopolizing control over all areas of a project.
☐ get angry when things are not achieved at my prescribed rate of accomplishment.
☐ forget to encourage my assistants.
☐ disparage others who are threatened by change or who don't have the gift of administration.

See 1 Corinthians 12:28; Titus 1:5.

The Gift of Apostle

A woman with the gift of apostle pioneers new territory for the kingdom of God, either planting churches or strengthening existing churches. She may work on the mission field or close to home. Her gift is a reflection of that given to the twelve in the early church, but it does not rival theirs. The gift of apostle is a blend of many gifts in action and carries authority in spiritual matters.

How many of these apply to you?

I tend to—

☐ feel drawn to provide organized worship and teaching where there is none available.
☐ feel drawn to help existing churches lay strong spiritual foundations.

- ☐ notice that other leaders turn to me for help.
- ☐ have many other gifts (for example, evangelism, shepherd/pastor, missionary, exhortation, faith, leadership, healing, miracles).
- ☐ find that people respect my character and authority.
- ☐ be able to work well with the men and women who serve with me.
- ☐ maintain a humble assessment of my role.

—

- ☐ become annoyed with slow progress.
- ☐ become over-eager to move on to new undertakings.
- ☐ become prideful or dictatorial.
- ☐ control other leaders instead of releasing them to serve in prominent positions.

See Ephesians 4:11; 1 Corinthians 12:28

The Gift of Celibacy

A woman with the gift of celibacy finds peace in being single and in having increased availability for Christian service. Although she may have numerous male friends, she chooses not to become romantically involved with them. Not all single women possess this gift. This woman may decide early in her life to remain unmarried (with or without a distinct sense of calling to this lifestyle) or she may choose to express this gift for the remaining years of her life after losing her husband.

How many of these apply to you?

+

I tend to—

- ☐ find my companionship with the Lord and with those whom I am called to serve.
- ☐ find joy in being single.
- ☐ find it possible to disregard my sexual needs.
- ☐ limit my social life to nondating situations.
- ☐ focus my energy on meeting the needs of others.

—

- ☐ sometimes become irritated with those who suggest I "find a partner."
- ☐ battle loneliness at times.
- ☐ become careless about my appearance or health and the impact this might have on others.
- ☐ sometimes feel angry with those who are busy with mates and families.
- ☐ become critical of people who will not commit as much time to Christian service as I do.

See Matthew 19:10-12; 1 Corinthians 7:7-9

The Gift of Deliverance

A woman with the gift of deliverance (exorcism) is empowered by the Holy Spirit to cast out evil spirits. She understands clearly that Satan is a strong but defeated enemy, a usurper who can be dislodged and removed from his evil strongholds by the authority of Jesus. As she uses this gift, this woman appreciates the importance of maintaining her personal relationship with God, growing in spiritual maturity, and praying for wisdom.

How many of these apply to you?

+

I tend to—

- ☐ have complete faith that victory over Satan's dominion has been won for us by Jesus.
- ☐ understand that people invite demonic trouble when they dabble in evil or yield to sin.
- ☐ exercise this gift with prudence.
- ☐ ask others to pray with and for me as I exercise this gift.
- ☐ recognize that I need the protection of spiritual oversight, guidance, and discipling.
- ☐ possess the gift of discernment of spirits; be able to differentiate between symptoms caused by organic problems or sin and a demonic presence.

—

- ☐ become overconfident because of previous successes, lapsing into using techniques that worked in other situations.
- ☐ fail to give God glory for my successes.
- ☐ become simplistic, blaming all ills on the devil or focusing on a few Scriptures about deliverance to the exclusion of the entire biblical message.
- ☐ criticize others whose approach to this subject differs from mine.

See Luke 9:1; Acts 8:5-8

The Gift of Discernment of Spirits

A woman with the gift of discernment of spirits is able to recognize right and wrong clearly. As with the gift of interpretation of tongues, she can interpret what she sees, hears, and reads, "just knowing" what is beneath the surface. She is able to determine what is of divine, satanic, or human derivation to a degree that is greater than that provided by a good grasp of Bible truth, ordinary sensitivity to the Holy Spirit, plain common sense, or trained critical faculties.

How many of these apply to you?

+

I tend to—

- ☐ realize that whatever is supernatural is not necessarily of God.
- ☐ know a true believer when I meet one.
- ☐ be able to identify what originates from God, humans, o the devil.
- ☐ be able to separate good from bad when they are mixed.
- ☐ spot lies, even when presented by a seemingly honest pe son.
- ☐ spot purity and truth, and endorse it.
- ☐ accurately predict the outcome of continued behavior whether it comes from good, bad, or mixed motives.

—

- ☐ sometimes believe I have all the answers.
- ☐ become proud of my ability to make judgments.
- ☐ rely too much on my own insight.

- ☐ expect other people to rely on my insights.
- ☐ present my perceptions harshly.
- ☐ perpetrate slander or cause division between believers.

See 1 Corinthians 12:10; Acts 16:16-18

The Gift of Evangelism

A woman with the gift of evangelism is able to bring people to faith in Christ. She has a passion to present the gospel message in a clear and compelling way. Although she knows the sorrow of seeing some people turn their backs on the Good News, she is not easily discouraged. Her greatest joy is to see someone respond to God's invitation to salvation through Jesus Christ.

How many of these apply to you?

I tend to—

- ☐ guide conversations toward God.
- ☐ be tireless and enthused about spreading the Good News.
- ☐ be able to present the gospel message clearly and confidently.
- ☐ be able to bring people to a point of decision about their commitment to Christ.
- ☐ know the joy of bringing a person to a saving faith in Christ.
- ☐ pray for those with whom I wish to share the gospel.
- ☐ seek training to better understand and present the gospel.
- ☐ encourage other Christians to bring people to Christ.

- ☐ quicken inside when I hear others share the Good News.
- ☐ feel deep sorrow for those who do not know Jesus as Savior.

—

- ☐ consider the gift of evangelism to be a higher gift than others.
- ☐ adopt a rote style of presentation and fail to perceive people's needs.
- ☐ become arrogant, failing to remember that conversion is the work of the Holy Spirit and not me.
- ☐ become boastful about the numbers I have led to Christ.
- ☐ browbeat those who have rejected the gospel.
- ☐ neglect to involve the new Christian in Christian fellowship.

See Ephesians 4:11; Acts 14:1; 21:8

The Gift of Exhortation (Encouragement)

A woman with the gift of exhortation has the spiritual capacity and desire to advise, admonish, and comfort others. People turn to her for help, sensing her ability to build them up. She is an active, not a passive, listener. She has a good understanding of human nature and a practical sense of how to apply scriptural truth to life.

How many of these apply to you?

I tend to—

- ☐ be a "people person"; I notice the emotional, spiritual, and mental needs of others and want to help.

- ☐ be an active, not passive, listener.
- ☐ be a good communicator.
- ☐ be a "magnet" for discouraged people, some of whom I barely know.
- ☐ be able to rebuke people when necessary.
- ☐ be decisive.
- ☐ be generally optimistic.
- ☐ be able to visualize a person's godly potential.
- ☐ recognize what steps need to be taken to help change lives.
- ☐ study the Bible for its practical application.

—

- ☐ be bored with subjects that do not apply to human lives.
- ☐ object when people with the gift of mercy don't seem to be firm enough with others.
- ☐ have little patience when people won't take the action I recommend.
- ☐ present "quick fixes," jumping in with solutions before listening long enough.

See Romans 12:6, 8; 1 Thessalonians 2:11-12

The Gift of Faith

A woman with the gift of faith is equipped by God with extra assurance that he is in complete charge and that he answers her prayers. Her trust in the Lord goes beyond a general affirmation of God's truth. Pressing against impossibilities, this woman's persevering certainty is contagious to others.

How many of these apply to you?

+

I tend to—

- ☐ have an intimate relationship with God.
- ☐ have others turn to me for prayers and assurance.
- ☐ remember to pray about matters both small and large.
- ☐ wait upon the Lord with perseverance and hope when I do not have answers.
- ☐ have an unquestioning confidence in God's sovereign love.
- ☐ be increasingly surrendered to God's will.
- ☐ encourage others to trust in God.

–

- ☐ expect others to possess an unrealistically high level of faith.
- ☐ suffer greatly if sinful behavior takes away my sense of closeness with the Lord.
- ☐ sometimes press ahead with baseless confidence before I have ascertained God's will.

See 1 Corinthians 12:9; 13:2; Acts 6:5

The Gift of Giving

A woman with the gift of giving can be rich or poor. She finds delight in giving money to others, preferring to give anonymously, if possible. If she is not able to give financial gifts, she donates her time and energy instead. Her satisfaction comes from enabling God's work to go forward.

How many of these apply to you?

+

I tend to—

- ☐ find joy in giving money to others.
- ☐ consider my resources to be “God’s money,” not “mine.”
- ☐ find creative ways to give financial aid.
- ☐ often give beyond a tithe of my income.
- ☐ be concerned more with contributing to the success of God’s work than with a return on my investment.
- ☐ be frugal for the sake of giving more.
- ☐ want to motivate others to be generous.
- ☐ become very attentive when the topic of giving is discussed.
- ☐ be motivated more by my own sense of where to give money than by appeals for contributions.
- ☐ be blessed by replenished resources that enable me to continue to be generous.

—

- ☐ give indiscriminately or wastefully.
- ☐ maintain such tight control over my money that I appear selfish to friends or family.
- ☐ become critical of how others give.
- ☐ slip into giving with mixed motives, perhaps using my gifts to manipulate situations or gain honor or approval.

See Romans 12:6, 8; 2 Corinthans 8:1-7; 9:6-8

The Gift of Healing

A woman with the gift of healing can pray for the sick and they will be healed by God's power. As an instrument of God's compassion, she understands that he does not choose to heal everyone. She may find particular success in praying for certain categories of physical, emotional, or spiritual needs.

How many of these apply to you?

+

I tend to—

- ☐ want to see God glorified through healings.
- ☐ have a gift of faith; I don't expect a sick person to furnish the faith necessary for healing.
- ☐ be willing to risk failure.
- ☐ resist letting others put me on a pedestal.
- ☐ be eager to join my healing prayers with those of other believers.

—

- ☐ take ownership of the gift as if I am the healer.
- ☐ exaggerate the results of healing prayers.
- ☐ become discouraged if my prayers are not answered.
- ☐ confuse my natural nurturing tendencies with God's compassion.
- ☐ propagate my own limited ideas about healing.

See 1 Corinthians 12:9, 28; Acts 5:15-16

The Gift of Helps

A woman with the gift of helps enjoys relieving others of routine duties. Indispensable to the smooth functioning of the church, she does not consider menial tasks to be beneath her. She prefers immediate tasks rather than the longer-term responsibilities that a woman with the gift of service might enjoy. Often a quiet, caring person, she serves without seeking glory.

How many of these apply to you?

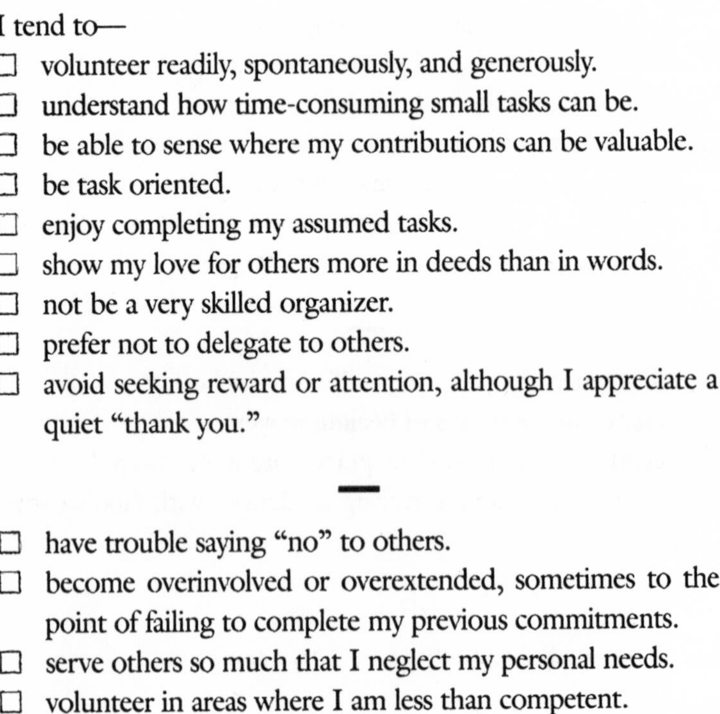

+

I tend to—

- ☐ volunteer readily, spontaneously, and generously.
- ☐ understand how time-consuming small tasks can be.
- ☐ be able to sense where my contributions can be valuable.
- ☐ be task oriented.
- ☐ enjoy completing my assumed tasks.
- ☐ show my love for others more in deeds than in words.
- ☐ not be a very skilled organizer.
- ☐ prefer not to delegate to others.
- ☐ avoid seeking reward or attention, although I appreciate a quiet "thank you."

−

- ☐ have trouble saying "no" to others.
- ☐ become overinvolved or overextended, sometimes to the point of failing to complete my previous commitments.
- ☐ serve others so much that I neglect my personal needs.
- ☐ volunteer in areas where I am less than competent.

☐ sometimes not let others help enough.
☐ sometimes feel weary and "used."

See 1 Corinthians 12:28; Mark 15:40-41

The Gift of Hospitality

A woman with the gift of hospitality shows Christ's welcoming love to both strangers and friends. She demonstrates genuine interest toward others and is generous with her time and her home, where people find a comfortable sense of belonging.

How many of these apply to you?

I tend to—
☐ feel comfortable opening my home for group meetings, social gatherings, and overnight guests.
☐ be eager to provide food for social gatherings.
☐ feel comfortable conversing with strangers and often prefer to reach out to those who are lonely instead of to my established friends.
☐ often find more fulfillment in serving guests than in being alone.
☐ invest time, energy, and money in caring for guests, without complaining.
☐ know how to make different kinds of guests feel comfortable, down to the small details.
☐ consider someone's interruption as an opportunity to serve that person.

- ☐ receive more compliments about the welcome in my home than about my housekeeping, even if my home is very beautiful.
- ☐ feel comfortable showing hospitality under humble circumstances.

—

- ☐ sometimes let my focus slip from showing God's love to "entertaining."
- ☐ fall into being competitive with my previous efforts, always trying to outdo myself.
- ☐ become critical of other women's efforts to show hospitality.
- ☐ want to monopolize the ministry of hospitality within my church.
- ☐ fall into using my gift to cater to friends only.
- ☐ spend so much time and money on hospitality that I neglect my family or fail to tithe.

See 1 Peter 4:9-10; Romans 16:23

The Gift of Intercession

A woman with the gift of intercession identifies with God's desires, praying every day for others, often at great length, with intensity and faith-filled confidence. She sees many answered prayers.

How many of these apply to you?

+

I tend to—

- ☐ feel drawn to pray for the needs of others.
- ☐ enjoy intercession—it's not a burden.
- ☐ be asked by others to pray with them or for them.
- ☐ recognize this gift in others and desire to band together with them for more effective intercession.
- ☐ have ever-increasing confidence that my prayers are heard and answered by God.
- ☐ have a set of prayer "assignments" (for example, church unity, needs of a certain ministry, particular individuals).
- ☐ notice that my ability to intercede is growing through the years of my life.
- ☐ (if I am older) notice that I am a more effective intercessor as I age.

−

- ☐ become too rigid about maintaining my prayer times, at the expense of relationships and other responsibilities.
- ☐ too quickly assure someone that prayer will solve everything.
- ☐ be unwilling to do work that isn't related to prayer.
- ☐ notice pitfalls or problems when I fail to operate "in the Spirit" (for instance, failing to keep commitments to pray, breaking confidences, trying to manipulate others by my prayer).

See 1 Timothy 2:1-2; Colossians 1:9-12

The Gift of Knowledge

A woman with the gift of knowledge applies scriptural insights to her life and to the lives of others with particular life-bringing freshness. She is often able to explain confusing scriptural concepts and can become a valuable resource for others. If her gift is blended with the gifts of prophecy and discernment, it may enable her to offer "words of knowledge," insightful revelations about others' needs that surpass human reasoning power or learning.

How many of these apply to you?

+

I tend to—

☐ delight in new insights into the Word of God.
☐ get information that seems to be straight from God.
☐ want to apply inspired information in a way that brings life to people.
☐ like to present my insights to others as clearly as possible.
☐ want to stimulate in others a hunger for biblical knowledge and the ways of God.
☐ get feedback from others that insights I have shared have gone straight to their hearts.
☐ appreciate the insights of others with this gift.

—

☐ sometimes become absorbed in one point or topic, to the exclusion of others.
☐ be tempted to think I have all the answers (becoming "puffed up"—see 1 Cor 8:1).

- ☐ become critical toward others who fail to meet my standards for the use of this gift.
- ☐ become impatient with those who do not understand my insights.
- ☐ forget to ask for God's wisdom in applying the truths he shows me.

See 1 Corinthians 12:8; 13:2; 2 Corinthians 11:6; Acts 5:1-11

The Gift of Leadership

A woman with the gift of leadership can grasp a clear vision for the future of a Christian group, formulate goals, and influence others toward the achievement of those goals. People trust her. Roles of leadership are conferred upon her, never seized at her initiative.

How many of these apply to you?

+

I tend to—

- ☐ see the "big picture."
- ☐ be able to articulate goals.
- ☐ be known for my integrity and wisdom.
- ☐ be able to identify the gifts of others that will contribute to an effort.
- ☐ be a good delegator.
- ☐ have the heart of a servant, not a dictator.
- ☐ work well with others and encourage unity of purpose.

–

- ☐ become proud of my position of power.
- ☐ become autocratic, denying the input of others.
- ☐ lose effectiveness if I forget to delegate responsibilities.
- ☐ lose impetus if I become bogged down in administrative details.
- ☐ criticize the weaknesses of those who work under me.
- ☐ neglect to encourage those who work under me.

See Roman 12:6, 8; 1 Timothy 4:12-16; 1 Thessalonians 5:12

The Gift of Martyr

A woman with the gift of martyr becomes a witness to God's truth in unsafe circumstances. She displays calm resolve while enduring great personal suffering, whether or not she is eventually killed for her faith. Her unusual attitude toward personal peril, while easy to mistake for foolhardiness, is based on complete confidence in God as the ultimate Victor.

How many of these apply to you?

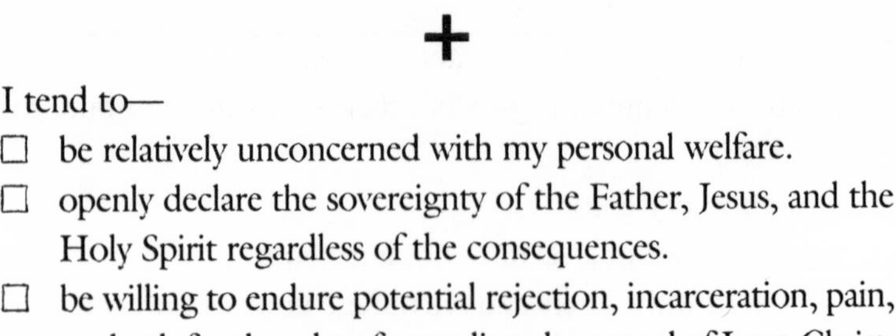

+

I tend to—

- ☐ be relatively unconcerned with my personal welfare.
- ☐ openly declare the sovereignty of the Father, Jesus, and the Holy Spirit regardless of the consequences.
- ☐ be willing to endure potential rejection, incarceration, pain, or death for the sake of spreading the gospel of Jesus Christ.

- ☐ volunteer for and persevere at work in inhospitable situations where other Christians are afraid to serve, including combat or disaster zones.
- ☐ be unintimidated at the prospect of living under a hostile foreign government.
- ☐ encounter rejection by family or others who consider my choices foolish.

—

- ☐ lose sight of God as my source, seeing myself as the primary warrior.
- ☐ lose sight of God's guidance, endangering myself unnecessarily.
- ☐ jeopardize the well-being of others.
- ☐ complain, or seek pity or public recognition for my suffering or efforts.
- ☐ become impatient with Christians who don't display the same courage I possess.

See 1 Corinthians 13:3; John 15:13; Hebrews 11:35

The Gift of Mercy

A woman with the gift of mercy is guided by her heart. She patiently attends to those who are lonely, burdened, needy, suffering, or dying, whether they are fellow believers or unbelievers. Not an advice-giver, she will empathize with others and look for simple, spontaneous ways to help.

How many of these apply to you?

+

I tend to—

- ☐ be nurturing in my prayers and actions.
- ☐ "rejoice with those who rejoice and weep with those who weep" (Rom 12:15, RSV).
- ☐ offer understanding without judgmentalism, when others might not know how to respond.
- ☐ dislike hearing others criticized.
- ☐ encourage others to express their emotions.
- ☐ be able to love the unloving or unlovely and seek opportunities to serve them.
- ☐ be attracted to caregiving fields such as medical services or missions.
- ☐ find special fulfillment in serving particular types of people (for example, the elderly, prisoners, the poor, the mentally ill, or the hospitalized).
- ☐ willingly give up my energy, time, and privacy for the sake of others.

—

- ☐ risk overinvolvement with others, sometimes helping so much that I prolong a state of helplessness.
- ☐ lack the discernment to distinguish valid needs from the apparent needs of people who should be rebuked, ignored, or helped by someone else.
- ☐ mistake my emotions of mercy for romantic love when dealing with men.
- ☐ neglect myself or ignore pressing personal obligations while reaching out to others.
- ☐ expect others to have my high level of compassion.

- ☐ know "where to stick the knife" if I'm angry with someone, because I understand their emotional weaknesses.

See Romans 12:6, 8; Matthew 25:34-40

The Gift of Miracles

A woman with the gift of miracles receives prayer answers that defy natural law as we understand it. Although miracles are relatively rare, a woman who has this gift will, over time, be able to identify several amazing events that have resulted from her faith-filled prayers. These marvels, which include more than physical healing or deliverance, bring glory to God, who sovereignly inspires them to authenticate his truth.

How many of these apply to you?

I tend to—

- ☐ have a high level of faith.
- ☐ recognize that God shows supernatural power through me, none of which originates in me.
- ☐ have confirmation from others that miracles have occurred.
- ☐ differentiate between true miracles and counterfeit ones, which bring no glory to God.
- ☐ recognize the miraculous in what others may call mere coincidence.

—

- ☐ take God's power for granted.
- ☐ falsely claim to have performed a miracle.
- ☐ draw attention to myself.

- ☐ try to produce a miracle by my own strength.
- ☐ denigrate basic, yet nonetheless miraculous events such as salvation, healing, or deliverance from evil strongholds.

See 1 Corinthians 12:10, 28, 29; Romans 15:18-19

The Gift of Missionary

A woman with the gift of missionary feels called to spread the gospel of Jesus to people of another culture. She may move to a foreign land or she may remain in her home region, possibly making short-term mission trips or helping local outreaches to people culturally unlike herself. She may offer behind-the-scenes support for other missionaries.

How many of these apply to you?

I tend to—

- ☐ yearn to reach out in a self-sacrificial way to people of other cultures or races.
- ☐ enjoy serving as a member of church missions programs.
- ☐ want to help missionaries through financial donations, encouraging correspondence, faithful intercession, or personal hospitality.
- ☐ use my professional skills in fields such as medicine, education, or agriculture to help people of another culture.
- ☐ want to learn a foreign language so I may effectively minister to the needs of others.

—

- ☐ bog down in my workload and lose sight of my first purpose—to present Jesus Christ.

- ☐ resent fellow Christians who do not share my missionary zeal.
- ☐ criticize other approaches to ministry in the mission field.
- ☐ adopt a condescending attitude, assuming that my standards are better than those of the people I serve.

See Ephesians 3:7-8; Acts 13:2-4

The Gift of Prophecy

A woman with the gift of prophecy declares God's will as she understands it. She may predict future events accurately, although she is more likely to proclaim truth in a way that edifies those who hear her, most of whom will be believers. She wants people to align themselves with God's will. She may "specialize" in her use of this gift, either in mode of delivery or in subject matter.

How many of these apply to you?

I tend to—

- ☐ consider what "God says" or "the Bible says" to be foundational to everything.
- ☐ want to convey to others an appropriate awe of the Lord.
- ☐ be unafraid of proclaiming the consequences of turning from the will of God.
- ☐ emerge from a crowd to defend the faith.
- ☐ be able to receive correction when I'm wrong. (I want God's truth to be proclaimed more than I want to be right.)
- ☐ find it difficult to soften my statements, even when corrected for being too blunt.

- ☐ notice that my predictive words are borne out in subsequent events.
- ☐ receive inspired dreams or visions.

—

- ☐ be too harsh, sometimes not taking mitigating circumstances into account.
- ☐ not know when to keep silent.
- ☐ become proud or domineering.
- ☐ lapse into thinking I have originated the truths I am sharing.

See Romans 12:6; Ephesians 4:11; 1 Corinthians 12:10, 28; 14:1-4

The Gift of Service

A woman with the gift of service enjoys handling practical aspects of Christian projects. She prefers commitments with known end points, normally seeking to accomplish one project before assuming another. Earnestly trustworthy, she may prefer to work alone. She herself does not want to assume overall administrative leadership of projects or committees although she is capable of organizing helpers.

How many of these apply to you?

I tend to—

- ☐ enjoy fellowship in the context of doing projects.

- ☐ prefer active tasks to passive ones such as listening or reading.
- ☐ find fulfillment when helping Christian leaders succeed in their projects.
- ☐ accept humble, behind-the-scenes, routine tasks, although I dislike repetition.
- ☐ contribute my own time, talent, and finances to projects, especially if it helps avoid red tape.
- ☐ do more than I'm asked to do.
- ☐ anticipate needs before they arise and recommend solutions.
- ☐ have a good memory for details in my project areas.
- ☐ be able to identify the abilities, gifts, and talents of others as they relate to my area of service.
- ☐ be more concerned with my task than with my rank or position in the church.

—

- ☐ volunteer too readily, sometimes overcommitting myself or my family/friends without asking them first.
- ☐ fail to complete projects or ministry goals due to overcommitment.
- ☐ not comprehend others' reluctance to serve.
- ☐ overidentify my self-worth with the project I am doing.
- ☐ become too possessive of my service.
- ☐ feel rejected or "used" when not thanked.

See Romans 12:6-7; 1 Peter 4:10-11

The Gift of Shepherd/Pastor

A woman with the gift of shepherd/pastor nurtures and protects other people's spiritual lives. She gathers them to herself, helps them find opportunities to learn about God, brings them to the larger fellowship, and protects them from spiritual harm. Her goal is to feed people with the Word of God and to help them become like Christ. She is undeterred by discouraging circumstances.

How many of these apply to you?

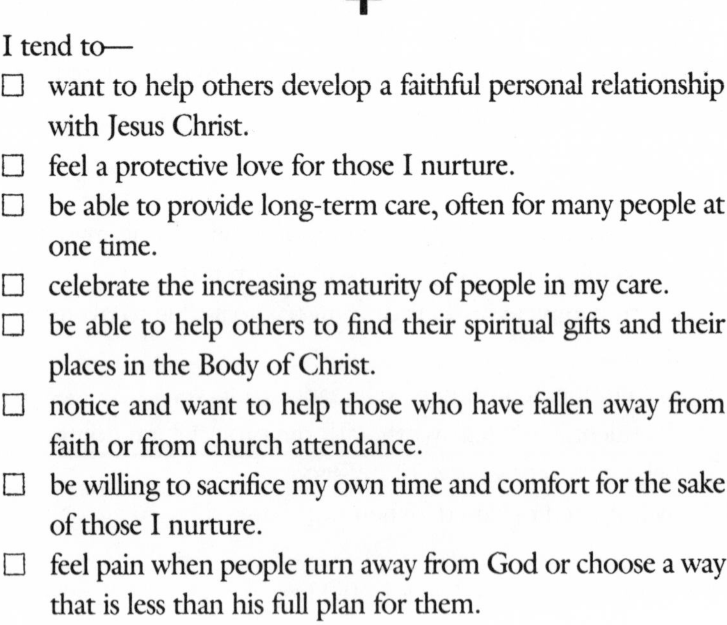

+

I tend to—

- ☐ want to help others develop a faithful personal relationship with Jesus Christ.
- ☐ feel a protective love for those I nurture.
- ☐ be able to provide long-term care, often for many people at one time.
- ☐ celebrate the increasing maturity of people in my care.
- ☐ be able to help others to find their spiritual gifts and their places in the Body of Christ.
- ☐ notice and want to help those who have fallen away from faith or from church attendance.
- ☐ be willing to sacrifice my own time and comfort for the sake of those I nurture.
- ☐ feel pain when people turn away from God or choose a way that is less than his full plan for them.

—

- ☐ keep "my flock" too dependent upon me.

- ☐ measure my self-worth in terms of the achievements or approval of those I nurture.
- ☐ become dictatorial, trying to control people's decisions out of a protective instinct.
- ☐ be indecisive because of fear of alienating those I nurture.
- ☐ be critical of the way others exercise their shepherding gift.

See Ephesians 4:11; 1 Peter 5:1-3

The Gift of Teaching

A woman with the gift of teaching seeks to understand and communicate the truth of the Bible. Her twin goals are to know and love God and to help others to do the same. The seeming drudgery of research and the recording of details are a delight to her.

How many of these apply to you?

I tend to—

- ☐ seek a church where the primary emphasis is teaching and learning about the Word of God.
- ☐ enjoy research and acquiring more knowledge about the kingdom of God.
- ☐ feel I can help others love God with their minds as well as their hearts.
- ☐ be intellectually sharp, even if not well-educated.
- ☐ find it easy to make truth come alive for others.
- ☐ be able to give detailed and well-supported answers to questions about the Bible.

- ☐ be quick to raise questions about teachings that do not agree with Scripture as I know it.
- ☐ want to continue to instruct others about Christian truth, even in the face of persecution or unusual limitations.
- ☐ express my gift not solely through classroom teaching, but in particular other ways (sermons, study groups, one-on-one, on television or radio, through writing, through drama, etc.).
- ☐ seek to learn how to be a better teacher.

—

- ☐ be tempted to follow too many "rabbit-trails" in my research or to overwhelm others with too many nonessential details.
- ☐ fail to apply the content of my teaching to my own life.
- ☐ fail to appreciate those who lack the gift of teaching.
- ☐ criticize other teachers or pastors.
- ☐ become too rigid in my opinions or too impressed with myself.
- ☐ be carried away by my own misunderstandings, ultimately spreading false teaching.

See Romans 12:6-7; Ephesians 4:11

The Gift of Tongues

A woman with the gift of tongues can speak in a "prayer language" that is granted to her and guided by the Holy Spirit. She has not learned it from anyone and she cannot understand it. If appropriate, she may use the gift in a public worship assembly, or she may use it only in her private prayer. If she speaks out in a public setting, Scripture states that someone should exercise the gift of interpretation of tongues (see 1 Cor 14:27-28 and definition below).

A woman with the gift of tongues can start or stop speaking at will. A wide variety of language-types or sound patterns is represented among those who possess this gift. Her prayer language can serve a variety of prayer functions, including but not limited to spiritual strengthening, praise, and intercession.

The Gift of Interpretation of Tongues

A woman with the gift of interpretation of tongues usually has the gift of tongues as well. In a public worship setting, she can often interpret an utterance in tongues into a language she knows (i.e., English in an English-speaking church). She cannot interpret an utterance in tongues if God does not give her that particular interpretation. Her interpretation conveys the tone or sense of the utterance in tongues and is rarely a word-for-word translation, because she has not studied the language she interprets.

A woman with this gift may also possess a gift of prophecy and may confuse the two. In time she will notice that interpretations tend to be most often exaltations of God and less often directive or corrective words from God. The validity of her interpretations is subject to the discernment of the members of the assembly, in particular those who possess the gifts of interpretation of tongues or of prophecy.

See 1 Corinthians 12:10, 30; 1 Corinthians 14:2-23, 26, 28

The Gift of Voluntary Poverty

A woman with the gift of voluntary poverty chooses to live a simplified life, unencumbered by physical possessions or by wealth. She considers these to be burdensome complications that inhibit or distract her from service to God. Whether she has known wealth or has come from humble circumstances, she has not been forced into poverty; her state is voluntary.

How many of these apply to you?

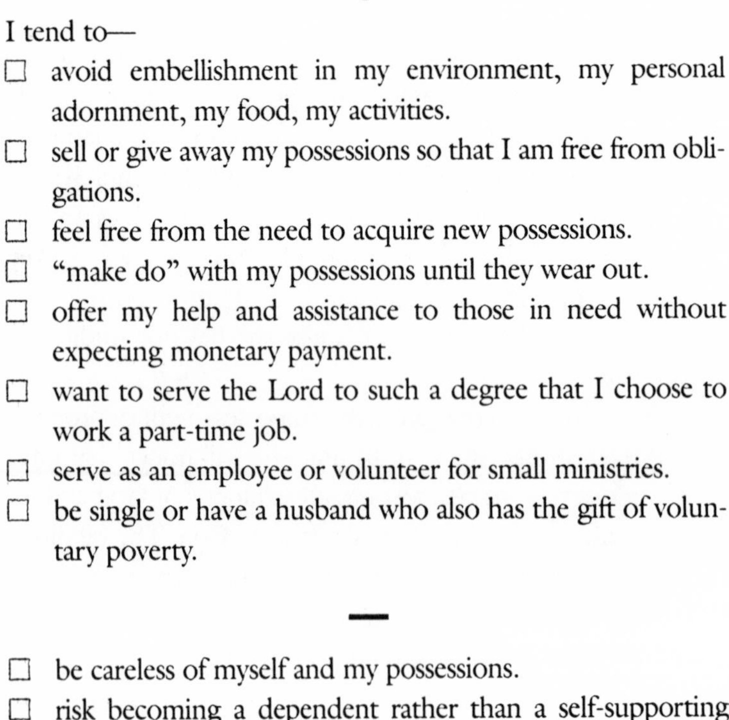

+

I tend to—

- ☐ avoid embellishment in my environment, my personal adornment, my food, my activities.
- ☐ sell or give away my possessions so that I am free from obligations.
- ☐ feel free from the need to acquire new possessions.
- ☐ "make do" with my possessions until they wear out.
- ☐ offer my help and assistance to those in need without expecting monetary payment.
- ☐ want to serve the Lord to such a degree that I choose to work a part-time job.
- ☐ serve as an employee or volunteer for small ministries.
- ☐ be single or have a husband who also has the gift of voluntary poverty.

—

- ☐ be careless of myself and my possessions.
- ☐ risk becoming a dependent rather than a self-supporting servant.

- ☐ choose poverty without adequate thought and prayer.
- ☐ be somewhat gullible about requests for help.
- ☐ isolate myself from the spiritual oversight and protective guidance of others.

See 2 Corinthians 6:3-4, 10; Acts 2:44-45

The Gift of Wisdom

A woman with the gift of wisdom is able to apply scriptural knowledge to real-life situations in a way that transcends human insights. Regardless of her education or other abilities, she is able to be a spiritual problem-solver. Her counsel consistently bears good fruit.

How many of these apply to you?

+

I tend to—

- ☐ understand that human wisdom is insufficient and often in opposition to God's wisdom.
- ☐ often remain quiet until others seek advice, appreciating that people can't receive it until they are ready.
- ☐ be involved in untangling difficult ethical or spiritual problems.
- ☐ pray for greater wisdom.
- ☐ humbly respect others who have this gift.

—

- ☐ criticize others who do not possess the accumulated insights I have gained.

- ☐ offer, instead of God's wisdom, my own opinions based on my prejudices or current trends.
- ☐ get carried away by successful ideas or solutions that are distorted or do not apply to the present.

See 1 Corinthians 12:8; 1 Corinthians 2:1-13

Notes

ONE
Eureka!

1. Leslie Flynn, *19 Gifts of the Spirit* (Colorado Springs, Colo.: ChariotVictor, 1974, 1994), 222.
2. Findley B. Edge, *The Greening of the Church* (Dallas: Word, 1971), 141, as quoted in C. Peter Wagner, *Your Spiritual Gifts Can Help Your Church Grow*, rev. ed. (Ventura, Calif.: Gospel Light, 1994), 117.
3. Adapted from Wagner, 157.
4. Bruce Bugbee, *What You Do Best in the Body of Christ* (Grand Rapids, Mich.:Zondervan 1995), 117.
5. "The concept of a questionnaire was originally published by Richard F. Houts (*Eternity*, May 1976, pp. 18–21) and later modified by C. Peter Wagner of Fuller Evangelistic Association." Paul R. Ford, *Unleash Your Church* (Pasadena, Calif.: Charles E. Fuller Institute, 1993), Appendix A.
6. It's worth noting that, although Wagner covers twenty-seven spiritual gifts in his books, the questionnaire itself tests for twenty-five of them. "Martyr" and "apostle" are omitted because their discovery doesn't lend itself to a question format.
7. Notably those by Marilyn Hickey, Don and Katie Fortune, and Women's Aglow Fellowship International, or Bruce Bugbee of Network Ministries International.
8. As defined by Bruce Bugbee and others.
9. Some of the best-known personality profiles are the Myers-Briggs Type Indicator and others based on it, administered professionally and available through Consulting Psychologist Press, Inc., 557 College Avenue, Palo Alto, CA 94306; the Carlson Personal Profile System (DiSC Test), administered professionally; The Taylor-Johnson Temperament Analysis, available from Psychology Publications, 5300 Hollywood Blvd., Los Angeles, CA 90027; and profiles based on the four personality types (sanguine, choleric, phlegmatic, melancholic) first identified by Hippocrates and other ancient Greek philosophers.
10. See Kevin Leman, *The New Birth Order Book* (Grand Rapids, Mich.:Baker, 1998). Originally published by Fleming H. Revell in 1984 as *The Birth Order Book.*
11. Wagner, 224.

TWO
Gifts Don't Come in Boxes

1. E.g., Marilyn Hickey, *Motivational Gifts* (Dallas: Word of Faith, 1983); and Don and Katie Fortune, *Discover Your God-Given Gifts* (Grand Rapids, Mich.: Chosen Books, 1987).
2. E.g., Don Basham, *A Handbook on Tongues, Interpretation, and Prophecy* (Pittsburgh, Pa.: Whitaker House, 1971). J. Oswald Sanders, *The Holy Spirit and His Gifts* (Grand Rapids, Mich.: Zondervan, 1940, 1970). "Gifts and Fruit of the Spirit," transcription of Assemblies of God Council forum (Springfield, Mo.: Gospel Publishing House, 1972).
3. E.g., Bugbee.
4. E.g., Wagner.
5. E.g., Flynn.
6. E.g., Arnold Bittlinger, *Gifts and Ministries* (Grand Rapids, Mich.: Eerdmans, 1973). Kenneth O. Gangel, *Unwrap Your Spiritual Gifts* (Wheaton, Ill.: Victor, 1983).
7. Corrie ten Boom, as quoted in Larry Christenson, *Speaking in Tongues* (Minneapolis, Minn.: Dimension, 1968), 5.
8. Other reputable teachers, including Paul R. Ford, prefer to designate some of these gifts as "probable gifts," for example celibacy, deliverance, hospitality, intercession, martyrdom, missionary, and voluntary poverty. He and other teachers include in their lists the gift of creative ability, as expressed through craftsmanship and music.

   (Just for interest: One of the earliest gift lists comes from a second-century Christian manuscript, *Acts of John*, which purports to be accounts of the acts of the apostle John. Chapter 106 of the work gives a "list of powers [*dynameis*]: wonders, healings, signs, charismata, teachings, governings, refreshments, services, knowledge, praises, graces, confidences, sharings." This list overlaps the lists we have in our canon of Scripture, but as you can see ["... praises, graces, confidences, sharings"] the list uses different terminology to highlight identifiable workings of the Holy Spirit. [Quoted in Stuart D. Currie, "Speaking in Tongues: Early Evidence Outside the New Testament," *Interpretation*, 19 (1965): 274–94. Reprinted in Watson E. Mills, *Speaking in Tongues: A Guide to Research on Glossolalia* (Grand Rapids, Mich.: Eerdmans, 1986), 83ff.])
9. Typical gift categories include, for example, **Service/Sign, Ordinary/Extraordinary,** (W.J. Conybeare and J.S. Hawson, *Life and Epistles of St. Paul* [Grand Rapids, Mich.: Eerdmans, 1949], chap. 13, as quoted in Donald Gee, *Spiritual Gifts in the Work of the Ministry Today* (Springfield, Mo.:Gospel Publishing House, 1963);

   Revelation/Power/Inspiration, (Gordon Lindsay, *Gifts of the Spirit* [Dallas: Christ for the Nations, n.d.]); **Intellectual/Word/Power,** (Robert

DeGrandis, S.J., *The Gift of Miracles* [Ann Arbor, Mich.: Servant, 1991], 30); **Motivational/Ministering/Manifestation** (Hickey); and **Speaking/Serving/Signifying** (Flynn). W.A. Criswell, in his book *The Baptism, Filling, and Gifts of the Holy Spirit* (Grand Rapids, Mich.: Zondervan, 1973), lists at least eight additional categorization systems of various scholar/teachers.

10. John Wimber and Kevin Springer, *Power Evangelism* (San Francisco: Harper & Row, 1986), 140–41. For further helpful discussion of the differences between Christian traditions in their approach to spiritual gifts, see Jack Deere, *Surprised by the Power of the Spirit: Discovering How God Speaks and Heals Today* (Grand Rapids, Mich.: Zondervan, 1993).
11. Michael Harper, *Gifted People: Discovering Your Supernatural Gifts and Learning to Use Them* (Ann Arbor, Mich.: Servant, 1990), 17.

THREE
Spiritual Gifts and You

1. Kenneth Cain Kinghorn, *Gifts of the Spirit* (Nashville, Tenn.:Abingdon 1976), 16.
2. Gee, 9–10.
3. Bugbee, 63.
4. Kinghorn, 34.
5. A.W. Tozer, *Tragedy in the Church: the Missing Gifts* (Harrisburg, Pa.: Christian Publications, 1978), 30.
6. Flynn, 15.
7. Wagner, 32.
8. Arnold Bittlinger, *Gifts and Graces: A Commentary on 1 Corinthians 12-14,* trans. Herbert Klassen & Michael Harper (Grand Rapids, Mich.: Eerdmans, 1967), 56.
9. Frank Laubach, as quoted in Bittlinger, *Gifts and Graces,* 57.

FIVE
Life Bearers

1. Pamela Smith, *Woman Gifts: Biblical Models for Forming Church* (Mystic, Conn.: Twenty-Third Publications, 1994), 71.
2. William McRae, *Dynamics of Spiritual Gifts* (Grand Rapids, Mich.: Zondervan, 1976), 48. R.E. Hedland and Mark Galli, articles devoted to William Carey in an issue of *Christian History,* 9, no. 4: 3, 17, 24–25.
3. Jean Daniélou, *The Ministry of Women in the Early Church* (Leighton Buzzard, Beds., England: Faith Press, n.d.), 19, 14. Translated from an

article by Glyn Simon in *La Maison Dieu,* no. 61 (1960).

4. Based on Roger Gryson, *Le ministére des femmes dans l'Église ancienne* (Belgium: Editions J. Ducolot), trans. Jean Laporte and Mary Louise Hall (Collegeville, Minn.: The Liturgical Press, 1976), 5.
5. Smith, 3.
6. Kenneth Scott Latourette, *Christianity Through the Ages* (New York: Harper & Row, 1965), 71. Richard M. Riss, "Who's Who Among Women of the Word," *Spread the Fire* (October, 1997): 9.
7. Danny Day, "Brutality Behind Bars," *Christian History* 16, no. 1 (1997): 39.
8. Kelvin D. Crow, "The Lady of the Lamp," *Christian History* 16, no. 1 (1997): 35.
9. Mary R. Schramm, *Gifts of Grace: Discovering and Using Your Unique Abilities* (Minneapolis: Augsburg, 1982), 36.

SIX
Into the Blender

1. Lindsay, 11.
2. Priscilla Dunning, *Gifts Don't Come in Boxes* (master's thesis, Regis University, 1986), 187.
3. Harold Horton, *The Gifts of the Spirit,* 9th ed. (Nottingham, England: Assemblies of God Publishing House, 1934, 1968), 146.
4. John MacPherson, *Commentary on St. Paul's Epistle to the Ephesians* (London: T. & T. Clark, n.d.), 311, as quoted in Gangel, 74.
5. Wagner, 111.
6. Criswell, 140.
7. John White, *When the Spirit Comes with Power* (Downer's Grove, Ill.: InterVarsity, 1988), 132.
8. Sanders, 109.
9. Andrew Murray, *Humility* (Springdale, Pa.: Whitaker House, 1982), 55.

SEVEN
Gifts in a Prison Camp

1. Sources: Oral account of Priscilla Dunning, with details corroborated by Kangmei Ren and by Go Puan Seng in *Refuge and Strength* (Englewood Cliffs, N.J.: Prentice-Hall, 1970); E. Bartlett Kerr, *Surrender and Survival: The Experience of American POWs in the Pacific in 1941–1945* (New York: William Morrow and Co., 1985).
2. Wagner, 61.

3. David B. Barrett, "Annual Statistical Table on Global Mission, 1997," *International Bulletin of Missionary Research* (January, 1997): 25, as quoted in *Family News from Dr. James Dobson* (September, 1997): 1, and in Wagner, 63.

EIGHT
Gifts From Country Club to Shantytown

1. Published by Thomas Nelson in 1979. Now available from the author at 2921 Plantation Road, Winter Haven, FL 33884. Further details were provided through a January, 1998, phone conversation with Wilma Stanchfield and from an article by Billie Ellis, "Being Struck by Lightning Reveals God's Love to Pair," in the *Winter Haven News Chief*, March 23, 1992.
2. Louise Perrotta, *All You Really Need to Know About Prayer You Can Learn From the Poor* (Ann Arbor, Mich.: Servant, 1996), 109–12.

NINE
Gifts, Against All Odds

1. John T. Wilkinson, ed., *Richard Baxter and Margaret Charlton: A Puritan Love-Story* (London: George Allen & Unwin, 1928), 118–19, as quoted in J.I. Packer, *A Grief Sanctified* (Ann Arbor, Mich.: Servant, 1998), 183.
2. E.M. Bounds, *Purpose in Prayer* (Grand Rapids, Mich.: Baker, n.d.), 148–50.

TEN
Gifts That Astound

1. Babsie Bleasdell with Henry Libersat, *Refresh Your Life in the Spirit* (Ann Arbor, Mich.: Servant, 1997), 84-85.
2. Wayne Grudem, as quoted in Deere, 66.
3. Alan Burgess, *The Small Woman* (Ann Arbor, Mich.: Servant, 1985), originally published by E.P. Dutton and Co. in 1957.
4. DeGrandis, 41.
5. Karen Burton Mains, *Open Heart, Open Home* (Elgin, Ill: David C. Cook, 1976), 46–47.
6. Agnes Sanford, *Sealed Orders* (Plainfield, N.J.: Logos, 1972), 259.

ELEVEN
Does God Sing Soprano?

1. Scholar Richard A. Baer, Jr., writes, "More and more I am impressed with the element of playfulness in glossolalia, the sheer childlike delight in praising God in this manner. It is a contagious delight, ... the freedom a child has to burst into laughter even at an important family gathering. It reflects a lack of pomposity, an ability to see oneself (even one's serious praying) in perspective." Richard A. Baer, Jr., "Quaker Silence, Catholic Liturgy, and Pentecostal Glossolalia: Some Functional Similarities," in Mills, 321.
2. Horton, 150.
3. George T. Montague, S.M., *The Spirit and His Gifts: The Biblical Background of Spirit-Baptism, Tongue-Speaking, and Prophecy* (New York: Paulist, 1974), 34.
4. Michael Sullivant, *Prophetic Etiquette: How to Avoid the Abuse of Prophetic Ministry* (Kansas City, Mo.: Metro Christian Fellowship, 1996), 9.
5. Jackie Pullinger and Andrew Quicke, *Chasing the Dragon* (Ann Arbor, Mich.: Servant, 1982). Quotes taken from pages 28-31.
6. Ché Ahn, *Into the Fire* (Ventura, Calif.: Renew/Gospel Light, 1998), 60–61.
7. Graham Cooke, *Developing Your Prophetic Gifting* (Kent, England: Sovereign World International, 1994), 194, as quoted in Ahn, 59–60.

TWELVE
Coming of Age

1. Boyd Luter and Kathy McReynolds, *Women as Christ's Disciples* (Grand Rapids, Mich.: Baker, 1997), 140–41.
2. Andrew Murray, *The Ministry of Intercession* (Springdale, Pa.: Whitaker House, 1982), 143.
3. *Today's Christian Woman* 20, no. 4 (July/August 1998): 39.
4. C.S. Lewis, *Letters to an American Lady* (Grand Rapids, Mich.: Eerdmans, 1975), 53.
5. Schramm, 84, 86.
6. Joyce K. Ellis, *The 500 Hats of a Modern-Day Woman* (Ann Arbor, Mich.: Servant, 1999), 180–81.
7. Elisabeth Elliot, "Women in World Missions," speech delivered to students at Urbana, Illinois, in 1973, and published as an essay in the book *All That Was Ever Ours* (Tarrytown, N.Y.: Fleming H. Revell, 1988), 171.

Resources

Books

Brown, Patricia D. *SpiritGifts: One Spirit, Many Gifts.* Nashville, Tenn.: Abingdon, 1996.

Bugbee, Bruce. *What You Do Best in the Body of Christ: Discover Your Spiritual Gifts, Personal Style, and God-Given Passion.* Grand Rapids, Mich.: Zondervan, 1995.

Deere, Jack. *Surprised by the Power of the Spirit: Discovering How God Speaks and Heals Today.* Grand Rapids, Mich.: Zondervan, 1993.

Flynn, Leslie B. *19 Gifts of the Spirit.* Colorado Springs, Colo.: ChariotVictor, 1994.

Ford, Paul R. *Getting Your Gifts in Gear.* Pasadena, Calif: Charles E. Fuller Institute, 1993. (See SEMINARS AND RETREATS for ordering information.)

Fortune, Don & Katie. *Discover Your God-Given Gifts.* Grand Rapids, Mich.: Chosen/Baker, 1987.

Gangel, Kenneth O. *Unwrap Your Spiritual Gifts.* Wheaton, Ill.: Victor, 1983.

Kinghorn, Kenneth Cain. *Gifts of the Spirit.* Nashville, Tenn.: Abingdon, 1976.

Kise, Jane A.G., David Stark, and Sandra Krebs Hirsh. *LifeKeys.* Minneapolis: Bethany House, 1996.

Wagner, C. Peter. *Your Spiritual Gifts Can Help Your Church Grow.* Ventura, Calif.: Regal/Gospel Light, 1994.

Catalog

LEADERSHIP ON THE EDGE: RESOURCES AND SEMINARS
Part of the ministry of the International Centre for Leadership Development and Evangelism, "Carrying on the legacy of pioneering evangelist Charles E. Fuller." Offers one of North America's largest selections of spiritual-gifts training resources of all descriptions, including varieties of gift tests and additional resources as they become available.

Leadership On The Edge
P.O. Box 41083 RPO South
Winfield, BC V4V 1Z7
Canada
(250) 766-0907
LeadEdge@bc.sympatico.ca
www.GrowingLeadership.com

Seminars and Retreats

PRISCILLA DUNNING
Seminars and Retreats
Distributor/facilitator of the Personal Profile System®
and DiSC™-related products

2727 Fletcher Avenue W
P.O. Box 16B
Tampa, FL 33618
(813) 960-2243
PrissD@aol.com

PAUL FORD
Books, Audiotapes,
Lay Mobilizing, Team Building, and Leadership Seminars
Workbooks:
The *Mobilizing Spiritual Gifts* series
Originally published through the Charles Fuller Institute of Evangelism
Presently available from
ChurchSmart
350 Randy Rd. #5
Carol Stream, IL 60188
1 (800) 253-4276
Fax: (630) 871-8708